ABRAHAM J. TWERSKI, M.D.

I'VE GOTTA GET OUT OF MY WAY!

ELIMINATING THE OBSTACLES TO SUCCESS

MEKOR PRESS

Menucha Publishers, Inc.
© 2017 by Rabbi Abraham J. Twerski
Typeset and designed by Beena Sklare
All rights reserved

ISBN 978-1-61465-424-7

No part of this publication may be translated, reproduced, stored in a retrieval system, or transmitted in any form or by any means, electronic, mechanical, photocopying, recording, or otherwise, without prior permission in writing from both the copyright holder and the publisher.

Distributed by:
Mekor Press
A division of Menucha Publishers
1235 38th Street
Brooklyn, NY 11218
Tel/Fax: 718-232-0856
www.menuchapublishers.com
sales@menuchapublishers.com

Printed in Israel

Contents

Introduction 5
The Problem Was Me.. 8
My Way Was Lying 13
I Heard, but I Didn't Listen 15
The "Way" Is Crucial 17
A Major Obstacle..19
Automatic vs. Manual Operation 22
The "Self" in Social Relationships 29
Are You a Victim of "Internal Terrorism"?................33
The Problem with a Pseudo-Identity 40
How Can I Be in My Own Way?................................. 44
But It's Only an Attitude 48
I Had to Get My Head Outta My Way 51
Why the Negative Self-Concept? 54
The Burnout Phenomenon 59
Will the Real Self Please Stand Up? 72
The Pitfall of Extremes 75
Getting out of God's Way.. 78
It's Hard to Believe 81
Alone or Lonely.. 85
Lying — the Greatest Obstacle 88
Complacency 94

Did He Really Have a Way?... 97
Abstinence Is Not Sobriety 101
Wholeness 103
Choosing What's Right 108
Chesed 111
Perspective 114
Staying Outta My Way... 116
No Torah-Secular Dichotomy 118
It Was Easier Back When.. 121
Preparing for the Future 126
Chronic Discontent 131
Control.. 137
Emunah 141
Which Way to Emunah?... 149
Obstacles to Emunah 155
Emunah is Truth 161
The Pursuit of Truth... 164
Levels of Emunah 167
To Learn from Everyone 171
Our National Weakness 175
Humility.. 177
The Indestructible Spark 178
Emunah in Hashem's Absolute Kindness 180
Hashem Will Provide 182
The Teaching of the Mahn... 184
Emunah in Hashem, Not in People....................................... 186
Precursors to Emunah 188
Rising from a Fall... 192
Chanan Got Outta His Way 194
Conclusion 198

Introduction

In the forty-plus years that I have been involved with treating recovering alcoholics and other addictions, they have taught me much about psychology and human behavior, much more than I learned in my psychiatric training. Many of the emotional problems that are found in the alcoholic can be found in most nonaddicted people. In the alcoholic, they are accentuated and very prominent, which makes them more easily identifiable. However, what we can learn from the alcoholic's recovery can be applied to other lifestyles that are counterproductive and sometimes frankly destructive. The following talk by a recovering alcoholic provided the insight that is the basis of this book:

> *For years, I was having problems, big ones and little ones. I couldn't find good solutions to these problems, or at least any that were of any duration. Eventually, I stopped looking for solutions and tried to escape from my problems by drinking.*
>
> *It seemed that nothing turned out the way I wanted it to because something was always getting in the way. That started almost right from the beginning of my marriage. Things would have been fine between my wife and me if my in-laws hadn't gotten in the way. Eventually, we moved away from them, and from a distance they were not as much of a problem, although they still managed to get between us.*

But even without the in-laws around, there were some problems at home. My lifestyle was pretty average. I liked to spend a lot of time with my friends and do different things with them, but my wife would get in my way. When the kids came around, I knew how to raise them and discipline them, but I couldn't do what I wanted with them because my wife would obstruct me. I would tell the kids one thing, and she would tell them another. It was very frustrating trying to be a good father when I had so much opposition. Also, my wife complained I was drinking too much, and she tried to keep me from drinking.

I built up a successful accounting firm, and I had several accountants working for me. I was the boss, and I set the tone for how things were to be done, but these guys who were working for me would get in my way. They wanted to use different methods from me. As my drinking increased, these guys who were working for me tried to take over the firm. They said that I was messing things up because of my drinking. I told them they were crazy. They said that they didn't want to break up the firm, but that I was to manage my own clients and not interfere with theirs, and they wouldn't touch any of my clients.

I actually welcomed this suggestion. With me doing my own work the way I saw fit, they wouldn't get in my way.

Things at home deteriorated, and my wife took the kids and went to her parents. I felt relieved, because now she wouldn't get in my way.

But now that I was free of anyone's interference both at home and at work, things didn't get better at all. In fact, things got much worse. One day my wife appeared at the office with my parents, not hers, and with the other men in the office. They insisted that I had to get help with my drinking. I didn't agree, but things were so messed up that I thought getting away for a few weeks couldn't hurt.

I ended up in an alcohol rehab place. After a while, and with a lot of help from the staff, I came to the realization that all the while that I'd thought I couldn't get things done because others were in my way, I was dead wrong. It wasn't the others who were in my way. I was in my own way. Even before I drank, it wasn't the wife or in-laws who were the obstacle, it was me. It suddenly hit me that if I wanted things to turn out right, I had to get out of my own way.

I must admit that I had never thought of it quite in these terms. Pogo said it, "I have met the enemy, and it is us." Many people who never drank may have the same problem. We get in our own way.

Why do we get in our own way? Probably because we are so preoccupied with ourselves that we cannot devote proper time and attention to other people and things. We may not be able to love others because we are too much involved with loving ourselves.

Let's look at some of the things that may cause us to focus unduly on ourselves, to the detriment of our relating to others or to our performance.

The Problem Was Me

There are different ways in which we can be the obstacle to success and happiness. I have often said that there seem to be four essentials to life: (1) food and water, (2) shelter, (3) clothing, and (4) someone to blame. If we can blame someone or something for our problems, we feel no obligation to make significant changes in our lives. Humans are creatures of habit, and making changes is uncomfortable. We may blame others for our being in a rut, attributing our problems to things we cannot change. That seems to let us off the hook. Here is one example.

Jeffery was thirty years old when he admitted himself to Gateway Rehabilitation Center for treatment. He had been a moderate marijuana user and had not used for six months, but he was unable to get on with his life. He had dropped out of college and was unable to hold on to a job. It appeared he had the "amotivational syndrome," one of the serious consequences of marijuana use by young people, who lose their motivation to do things and drift aimlessly. When they wake up, they realize that they wasted the most productive years of their lives.

Jeffery completed the treatment program successfully. Several months later he called, asking if he could spend the latter days of Pesach with me. He told me that even after treatment, he had not been able to move on in life. He said his problem was Elaine. In college, he had fallen in love with Elaine, who came from a Reform Jewish family. Jeffery had influenced her to become Torah observant, much to her father's chagrin. When she told her father that she wanted to marry Jeffery, he said, "Over my dead body!" Elaine could not stand up against her father, and she broke off the relationship with Jeffery. This had happened five years earlier, and Elaine had since married. "I can't get over losing Elaine," Jeffery said. "I'm still very much in love with her. I just can't get on with my life. I can't detach from Elaine."

I told Jeffery that he was not the first person in the world to lose a love relationship, and that the normal reaction is to go through a period of grief over the loss and then move on, and that there must be some reason why he was unable to do so. We spent some time trying to analyze why he was still stuck in this relationship. Elaine was now married and beyond reach. It was really no different from losing a loved one by death. One grieves for a period of time, then moves on, accepting the reality.

On Pesach afternoon, I took my siesta. I have learned to relax and transport myself back in time to my childhood, to the summers we spent in a cottage at Big Cedar Lake, Wisconsin. My days were all fun, from the time I awoke until bedtime. We either played baseball; went swimming, fishing, or hiking; played cards or Monopoly; or read comic books. I didn't have a worry in the world. Countless times, I have revisited Big Cedar Lake in my trance to reexperience that idyllic time.

During my siesta, I went back to Big Cedar Lake and relived an experience I had never recalled before. I used to love to row a boat, but at age nine, I was not allowed to row unless there was an adult with me. However, because I loved to row, I would get into the boat while it was tethered to the pier with a thick rope and row to my heart's content, fantasizing that I would discover a new continent on the other side of the lake (although I had already been there and all that was there was Gonring's Resort). Because I was tied to the pier, there was no danger in my rowing. If the boat were detached from the pier, I might row to the middle of the lake, which would have been dangerous.

I awoke from my siesta and realized I had dreamed the solution to Jeffery's problem. Jeffery was suffering from low self-esteem and had no self-confidence. Consequently, he was afraid to do anything that might result in failure. Doing anything at all, whether going to college or holding a job, presented the risk of failure. But Jeffery did not recognize this as the problem. To explain to himself why he was unable to move on, he blamed it all on the loss of Elaine. As long as he was wallowing in this grief, he did not have to fault himself for his inactivity. Furthermore, since Elaine was beyond reach, this excuse could last a lifetime. He was a victim, and he indulged in a pity party. "Poor me! I lost my beloved Elaine. I am doomed to a life of misery."

Jeffery did not concoct this idea. He did not have to, because his subconscious mind did it for him. He had no idea that this is what was happening to him. The subconscious mind is very clever and very resourceful. When it sees that a person is in distress, it tries to protect him from the pain by using one or more of its defensive tactics. It really doesn't care that the defense may be counterproductive.

What was really Jeffery's pain? It was his anxiety, his fear of failure, and if he were aware of this, he would have to confront this fear and do something about it. So his subconscious essentially said to him, "You're not afraid of failure at all. You've been paralyzed by this terrible thing that happened to you." As long as Jeffery could consider himself an unfortunate victim, deprived of his beloved by an irascible father, he did not have to look at himself.

The subconscious mind's ability to deceive us by rationalization is colossal. We believe what it tells us because it relieves us of anxiety. Unfortunately, as in Jeffery's case, it threatened to ruin him forever.

We are all subject to rationalizations. We may not know the real reason why we do or refrain from doing something. If knowledge of the real reason would be unpleasant, the subconscious blocks the real reason from our awareness, and it substitutes a logical, albeit untrue, reason. That is what rationalization is: substituting a *good, logical* reason in place of the *true* reason.

Furthermore, the nature of all matter, animate and inanimate, is *inertia*. We must be motivated to make the effort to overcome inertia. Our subconscious may allow us to stay comfortable, doing nothing and not feeling guilty about it. It may "tie us to a pier," as it were, so that we may feel helpless. We think that we really want to move ahead. It's just that we can't, because we are tied to something from which we cannot detach.

The way to avoid this self-defeating defense is to overcome the fear of failure and to get help with our anxieties. As you may guess, this fear is grounded in low self-esteem. A person with good self-esteem knows that there are failures in life, and while a failure is indeed very unpleasant, it need not be devastating. If we fail, we lick our wounds and try to see what we can do to avoid failure next time. A person with low self-esteem cannot tolerate failure, and the subconscious mind sees to it that he does not have to — by convincing him that he is a victim of circumstances.

There is not too much we can do about the subconscious mind's defensive maneuvers. Physiologically, if bacteria enter our body, the body reacts by implementing the immune system and producing white blood cells to destroy the bacteria. These are automatic responses, which we do not initiate. The psychological defenses are quite similar. They are autonomous and function beyond our awareness. While we may not be able to control these defenses, we can do something about the reason why the defenses are set in motion, and that is by building up our self-esteem and developing an attitude toward life that will enable us to avoid becoming anxious when circumstances are difficult.

My Way Was Lying

When I assumed the directorship of the St. Francis Hospital Department of Psychiatry, I inherited an alcohol detoxification unit. I was totally unprepared for this. Four years of medical school and three years of psychiatric training did not provide any teaching of addiction, although a huge portion of any doctor's clientele, even at that time, had some type of addiction. A veteran recovering alcoholic, who conducted the weekly AA meeting on the unit, was my first instructor. One of the first things he taught me was, "You can always tell when an alcoholic is lying about his drinking just by watching his face. If he's moving his lips, he's lying." I found that this was equally true of other addictions.

We start the habit of lying early in childhood, to escape punishment and blame. The problem is that in early life, we often get away with it, and the imprint on us is that lying works. Recent history has demonstrated the folly of covering up our mistakes, and even the power of the presidency can't protect a president from being displaced from office. When I lecture to medical students, I advise them to admit their mistakes. Many patients and their families will forgive even a serious mistake, but if one denies it, the patient's lawyer will call in an expert to review the case, and no mercy is shown if the physician tried to deny and cover up his mistake.

That one stands to gain by lying is wrong. While there may be a short-term gain, there is a long-term loss. This is beautifully taught by the Midrash, which relates that when Noach built the ark and gathered survivors, *sheker* came along and wanted entrance. Noach told him that only couples may be admitted to the ark, and that he should find a mate. He met *schlemazel*, who was also looking for a mate to gain access to the ark. They formed a partnership whose terms were that whatever profit *sheker* makes will always go to *schlemazel* (*Tanchuma, Noach*). And that is how things have continued throughout history: anything gained by *sheker* ultimately ends up by *schlemazel*.

Honesty and truthfulness are not only ethically correct, they are also most expeditious. Yet our childhood habits of denying our mistakes are tenacious, and lying is a most destructive trait. One drug addict said, "Stopping to use drugs was very hard, but stopping to lie was much harder."

A wise father said to his children, "If you do something wrong, I may have to discipline you, but I will forgive you. However, if you lie about it, I will not forgive you."

Lying to others is ethically and morally wrong, but lying to oneself is simply stupid. Yet that is what happens when one procrastinates. If a person decides that he will not do a particular thing, his decision may be right or it may be wrong. But if he says, "I will do it, but just not now," he is lying to himself. *Mesillas Yesharim* says there is nothing as dangerous as procrastination because by procrastinating, one is lying to oneself.

I Heard,
but I Didn't Listen

The person cited in the introduction had been blaming all his problems on others. Closely related to this trait is looking for the faults in other people, although one does not blame one's problems on them.

One recovering person said, "I was always noticing the character defects in other people. This guy is a hothead. He blows up at any trifle. This other guy is a tightwad. This guy is a show-off and a name-dropper. He wants you to think he's an important person, although I don't know why. This guy is a blabbermouth. That guy is a know-it-all. When I got involved in the 12-step program, I was told I must do a *personal moral inventory* and stop taking everyone else's inventory. It has made a great difference in my personality and behavior."

It is interesting that in the introductory prayer in the morning we read, "Help me to see the virtues of my fellow men and not their shortcomings." This attitude is conducive to proper *kavanah* in *tefillah*. The Baal Shem Tov cited the verse in *Tehillim* (121:5), "Hashem is your shadow at your right hand," and he explained that a person's shadow mimics his every move. If one lifts his hand, the shadow does likewise. Thus, if a person does not focus on other people's faults, Hashem will not focus on his faults. It is much to our advantage to ignore people's shortcomings, because then Hashem will ignore our shortcomings.

The motivation for focusing on other people's faults is probably because it decreases our perspective of our own faults. The Baal Shem Tov said that "the world is a mirror." Inasmuch as we are generally blind to our own shortcomings, Hashem arranges that we should notice them in others. Hence, the defects we see in others are precisely those we have ourselves, thus anticipating the modern psychological mechanism of *projection*.

I heard these ideas, but I did not listen to them. I have become a much easier person to get along with once I got outta my way of passing judgment on other people.

The "Way" Is Crucial

While individual acts are important, a person's "way" is more comprehensive and represents how a person thinks and feels, and it is the personality and character that gives rise to one's acts.

It is of note that when the Israelites in the desert committed the grave sin of the Golden Calf, Hashem said to Moshe, "Go, descend, for your people that you brought up from Egypt have become corrupt. *They have strayed quickly from the way that I have commanded them.* They have made themselves a molten calf, prostrated themselves to it...and they said, 'This is your God, Israel'" (*Shemos* 32:7-8).

Hashem prefaced the sin of idolatry with, "They have strayed quickly from the way that I have commanded them." It is not only the idol worship that is wrong, but also "straying from the way I commanded them."

What is the "way" that Hashem commanded them? This was told to them at Sinai, "You shall be to Me a kingdom of ministers and a holy nation" (*Shemos* 19:6). A holy person is apart from others because he tries to remove himself from the temptations that drag human beings down from the estate to which they should aspire.

The secular world operates according to the idea, "If it feels good, do it." There is nothing wrong with enjoying the good things in this world. The *berachah* we recite in the spring when the fruit trees blossom is, "Blessed are You, Hashem, King of the universe, for nothing is lacking in His universe, and He created in it good creatures and good trees *to cause mankind pleasure with them.*"

It is also written (end of *Kiddushin, Talmud Yerushalmi*) that one of the questions we will be asked on our Judgment Day is, "Did you enjoy My world?" But that is a far cry from the hedonistic viewpoint that considers the world to be a huge amusement park, with no goal in life other than "Eat, drink, and be merry, for tomorrow you die."

One might think that Torah observance is the perfect antidote to a hedonistic lifestyle. Some eight hundred years ago, Ramban coined the term *naval b'reshus haTorah* — a person who is in technical compliance with all of Torah yet is a physically indulgent scoundrel. Some *frum* people seem to have adapted the hedonistic mantra of, "If it feels good *and it's kosher,* do it." This is a frank violation of *"kedoshim tihiyu"* (*Vayikra* 19:2). Yes, enjoy Hashem's world — but like a mensch, not like an animal.

A Torah Jew must have a *derech* that enables him to be *kadosh*.

A Major Obstacle

This may appear contradictory, but the *sifrei mussar* ascribe great importance to *bittul hayesh*. I am not happy with translating *bittul hayesh* as "self-effacement," but I have not found a better translation. *Bittul hayesh* may be best understood as the opposite of "narcissism." The latter is a condition in which a person's ego is out of sight. He thinks himself to be the greatest and expects everyone to recognize it and treat him accordingly. *Bittul hayesh* is not only humility, it's also realizing that one's importance in existence is solely to fulfill the mission for which one was created, which is to develop spirituality and become close with Hashem.

The self-consciousness of the narcissist is, in fact, a kind of mental illness. Think for a moment about where your ears are, then your eyes, then your throat. If you do not make it a point to think of them, you would not be aware of them. That is, as long as you are healthy and they are functioning well. If something does call your attention to them momentarily, they quickly slip back into unawareness. But if you have an earache or sore throat, or your vision is blurred and you see spots in front of your eyes, you become *very* aware of these parts of our body. In fact, you may hardly be able to think of anything else.

One of the difficulties with the concept of *bittul hayesh* is that there is a *yesh* that one must be *mevatel* (reduce, eliminate, or negate). One is conscious that one exists, and one must rid oneself of that feeling.

When one is *mevatel* chametz before Pesach, it is as though it is nonexistent. One does not think, *I do own chametz, but I dismiss it. I put it out of my mind*. Since it is forbidden to own chametz, *bittul* renders it nonexistent. That is the desirable *bittul hayesh*. One is not conscious that one has a self that one must be *mevatel*.

Being conscious of part of your body generally means that there is something wrong with it. It either hurts or is not functioning properly.

What is true of part of your person is true of all of it. If you are emotionally well and functioning optimally, you don't think about yourself for more than a fleeting moment. If you are conscious of yourself for a longer period of time, it is because — like your ears, eyes, and throat — there is something emotional that is not completely well or is not functioning optimally.

If you have severe ear pain, chances are this occupies your attention so much that you cannot attend very well to other things, whether work or relating to other people. You may ask for time off work or apologize to people because you cannot relate well to them. Much the same may happen when it is you *yourself* that is uncomfortable.

To the degree that you focus on yourself, to that degree you may be distracted from work or other people.

However, in contrast to physical pain, you may be unaware that you are being drawn to focus on yourself. Consequently, you may not even be aware that you are not functioning up to par. You may keep on working, but you are not at your best performance. You interact with people, but not as smoothly as you would like.

The *sifrei mussar* give great importance to *anivus*. This is simply good mental health, and it enables you to function optimally.

Automatic vs. Manual Operation

We can see why self-consciousness is troublesome by looking at an extreme case.

Take, for example, a person who is paranoid. I am not referring to *paranoid schizophrenia*, where someone hears voices and thinks that there is a conspiracy to kill him. That is an obvious case of mental illness. Rather, I am referring to a person who has a *paranoid personality*. He has an uncomfortable feeling that people may be staring at him and that people are picking on him. He feels that he is the center of attention in a negative way.

He is extremely self-conscious.

This is also true of the polar opposite. A person may feel that he is being totally ignored. No one is noticing his presence. No one is looking at him. It is as if he did not exist. This is a feeling of inferiority, which is psychologically unhealthy, and, again, is characterized by severe self-consciousness.

A person who is in good emotional health and thinks well of himself is not likely to be concerned whether or not people are looking at him. It makes no difference to him whether they notice him or not. The Torah relates that the spies Moshe sent to scout Canaan reported, "We saw there the

Nephilim, the sons of the giant. We were like grasshoppers in our eyes, and so we were in their eyes" (*Bamidbar* 13:33). One of the commentaries faults them for being influenced by what others thought of them. On the other hand, people with feelings of inferiority may do things to attract attention and to make themselves more conspicuous.

The more intense the feelings of inferiority, the more extreme are the attention-getting mechanisms.

Having suffered from unwarranted feelings of inferiority since childhood, I am well aware of the *shtick* I did to be noticed. I'm sure that at times I made a fool of myself, but better that than be a nobody.

People who are confident of their ability to function do whatever they are doing with their full attention to the task at hand. People who are unsure of themselves may be concerned about possibly making a mistake and what that would do to them. They may be so preoccupied with themselves that they become distracted. Unfortunately, such distraction may divert their full attention from what they are doing and may bring about the very mistake they fear making. This often occurs in perfectionists.

A person who is self-conscious and is worried about what would happen if he made a mistake may not be able to shake off his self-consciousness. I was consulted by a nineteen-year-old college student who was doing poorly in his courses. This was surprising to him, because he had been an excellent student throughout high school.

It turned out that he came from a coal-mining town, where everyone in the family worked in the coal mines. Most of the people began working in the mines at a young age. Some had not finished high school. No one in his extended family had gone on to college. His father boasted that his son was the first of the clan to go to college. His father made no secret of the sacrifice he was making to put his son through college, but it was all worth it because of the honor the young man would bring to the family.

This young man indeed felt that he was carrying the family honor on his shoulders. Although he studied well and absorbed the material, his mind would become a total blank when he took an exam. He could have easily passed the exam if the only challenge was to get a good grade. But there was much more riding on his performance. If he did not do well, he would be disappointing his father, who was sacrificing so much for his education. He would be letting the whole family down. His anxiety over this paralyzed his thinking. The fear of the consequences of failing made him fail. There was no way he could shake himself loose from this feeling.

Much the same happens when a person's pride is at stake. The dread of making a mistake can so interfere with the performance that it precipitates a mistake.

I refer to this as the "William Tell syndrome," based on the story of William Tell, who was an expert archer. He had somehow run afoul of the king, and the latter ordered him to shoot an arrow at an apple perched on Tell's son's head. The story goes that Tell succeeded at the challenge but that anyone with less expertise and confidence than Tell, even if he could accurately hit the bullseye of a target, would be so anxious at shooting an arrow at an apple perched on his son's head, that his hands would be tremulous and he would be doomed to fail.

Excessive self-consciousness can result in bizarre behavior. When I did psychiatric evaluations for the prison, a young man was brought for an examination. He had been arrested in a bungled attempted bank robbery. His father was a self-made man who had gone from rags to riches by his work and business acumen. The son felt himself totally dwarfed by his father's success and that he had very meager accomplishments of his own. When he entered the interview room, he smiled and said, "Hello, doctor. Did you see my picture on the front page of the newspaper today?" He had finally succeeded in calling attention to himself. The motive for the bank robbery may have been more for being noticed than for the money.

Do you remember the school clown, the kid who was forever getting kicked out of class because of his antics? Do you remember how he smiled when the teacher made him leave the room? That was a smile of triumph. Thirty kids plus the teacher were all focusing on him! As I recall, the class clown was not a stupid kid. He could have achieved positive recognition by excelling in his studies. But because he did not think he was bright enough to excel academically, he chose the negative road to prominence.

People who are not self-conscious have no need to draw attention to themselves. They generally do not think about themselves. The "self" takes care of itself "automatically."

There are two ways for a mechanism to operate: manually or automatically. When a machine runs on automatic, you leave it alone and it performs its function. On manual, however, you have to direct its function. Automatic is not only easier than manual, it is also more efficient. On manual it is much more likely that one may make a mistake.

The Torah relates that Adam and Chava were punished for eating the forbidden fruit of the tree whose fruit enabled man to distinguish good from bad (*Bereishis* 2:9). As a result of their sin, "the eyes of both of them were opened and they realized that they were naked" (ibid. 3:7). Rambam asks, "It would appear that gaining insight is a reward rather than a punishment," and he explains that prior to the sin, man operated by instinct rather than by intellect, like all other creatures. Instinct is far more efficient than intellect, which is subject to distortion and misinterpretation.

The human being operates on both levels. We do not think about our breathing. That is run automatically by one of the centers in the brain. Sure, we could take over and do our breathing on manual, thinking, "Inhale...now exhale. Inhale...now exhale." If you did that, you would not have your mind free to do anything else. Furthermore, the automatic control center knows when it is necessary to increase your respiration, such as when you exert yourself, in order to bring more oxygen into the system. On manual, you would not know just how fast you should be breathing at any given time. In His infinite wisdom, Hashem delegated breathing to the automatic control center.

This is also true of blinking, which is necessary to keep the cornea from drying out. Can you imagine what it would be like if you had to control your blinking consciously or if you had to think about walking? "Lift the left foot and put it forward. Now bring the right foot forward and put it in front of the left foot." Not only would we not be able to do anything else, but we would probably go insane trying to control our breathing, blinking, and walking.

So Hashem did the wise thing. He put those functions that are necessary for life under automatic control. We may at times take over for a short while and change the rate of our breathing or blinking, but for the greater part of our lives, these functions proceed automatically and efficiently.

Those functions that are not essential to preserve life and health are done manually. You do not write a letter or cook a roast automatically. You think about what to write or what ingredients to add. You look at the container to make sure it is onion powder and not cinnamon that you are putting on the roast meat. Hashem assigned these to our conscious control. He trusted you to check the ingredients, because in the worst scenario, cinnamon on the roast is not tasty, but it is not fatal. But improper breathing can have very grave consequences, so He put it under automatic control.

Here is more evidence of the superiority of automatic over manual function. Golf pros give lessons on how to play golf. They teach you how to grip the golf club, how to stand, where to keep your head during the swing, and how far your right heel should be off the ground, among other things. When you try to put all these teachings into action, you don't exactly come up with a stellar performance. Why? Because when you have to follow all those directions, you're on manual. Your swing has the grace of a mechanical tin soldier. The poise and graceful movements of the golf pros are due to the fact that they *don't* think about all these things. It comes naturally to them. They function on automatic. Of course, the more you practice what you've been taught, the more automatic your playing becomes, and you can improve your score. But as long as you have to use manual, your score will suffer.

What about the "self?" Except for special circumstances, the self should run on automatic, without your attention being directed toward it. That will allow you to function smoothly. If, for whatever reason, you take the self out of automatic and direct it manually, you will have the same inefficiency as if you controlled your breathing automatically.

Even if one cannot operate totally on automatic, there is great benefit in decreasing the degree of manual control.

The less one does manually, the easier one's life can be.

Let's look a bit further into the effects of manual vs. automatic in a variety of conditions. Then let's see how we can increase the automaticity by reducing the self-consciousness.

The "Self" in Social Relationships

Have you ever had an instructor whom you felt was not as interested in sharing information with you as he was in impressing you with how much he knows? On the other hand, can you recall teachers who were really interested in your gaining knowledge and were not trying to impress you? Whom do you remember fondly? From whom did you learn best?

Teachers are certainly not the only people who may try to display their knowledge. This is a rather prevalent trait. There are name-droppers who appear desperate to impress us with their importance. Some people do not make it as obvious as name-droppers, yet we feel that their primary motivation in conversing with us is to demonstrate how much they know. Because the conversation has more to do with ego than with sharing knowledge, these people are reluctant listeners. You may have something valuable to tell them, but they are too preoccupied with their ego and with impressing you to be open to learning something.

I can recall teachers who were excited when I told them something they did not know. They did not try to impress anyone with how much they knew. They were truly humble.

Their efforts to impart knowledge were sincere, and this is why I learned so much from them. Much the same is true of my acquaintances. Some people I know are not really interested in me other than that I am someone whom they hope to impress with their importance.

Let's not confuse the "self" with selfishness and the "non-self" with altruism. Most of what we do is directed toward self-gratification of one kind or another. Self-interest is normal. Self-interest turns into reprehensible selfishness only when one wishes to gratify oneself without any consideration of what that may do to someone else. It is the lack of consideration for other people's rights and feelings that we condemn as being selfish. Eating a tasty food is "selfish" in that it is self-gratifying, but there is nothing wrong with that because it does not harm anyone else. If, however, there is barely enough food to go around and I take more than my fair share, then I am being what we generally refer to as selfish.

A person who desires my friendship because it pleases him in some way is not being selfish. Quite the contrary, it makes me feel good that someone desires my companionship. I enjoy helping friends, and I actually welcome their requests for a favor. They are not exploiting the relationship. But when someone wishes to associate with me only so that he can tell me how great he is, I see that as exploitation. These are not the kind of associations that I desire.

Sometimes we must tolerate such exploitation. If I wish to sell a product or service to someone, I stand to better achieve this if I can make the prospective buyer happy. He may wish to tell me about his great accomplishments. If I wish to land the contract, I may have to listen to stories about his proficiency in fishing or other heroic feats. That is expedience, but I certainly do not enjoy it.

Hopefully, reading this book will enable you to see how and where your "self" is intrusive and what you can do to develop a nonintrusive, healthy "self" that will give you as little concern as your healthy eyes and ears. But you should be aware that many people have not achieved a healthy "self." When they interact with you, they may be very conscious of their "self." They may feel you are studying them and they may be anxious that you might discover one or more of their defects. In a good friendship, people may lower their guard. They may think you know them well enough, and they're not concerned that you may discover something about them that would turn you off. But in many social contacts, the relationship is far less secure.

When you come into any gathering, watch how rigid many people are. You can sense their defensiveness and how cautious they are in their speech and movements. It is easy to observe how people act so that they appear important. Of course, if this is a reception at which liquor is being served, the defensiveness may disappear as they become a bit anesthetized. Self-consciousness is a feeling, and when alcohol is consumed and feelings are numbed, self-consciousness melts away.

In relationships other than close friendships, you'll put people at greater ease if you allow yourself to be impressed. They will be eminently grateful if you appreciate their importance. And because you will have a healthy "self," you will have no need to impress them.

Ironically, by not trying to impress them and by allowing them to demonstrate their importance, you will have made the greatest possible impression upon them. Precisely because you allowed them to tell you how great *they* are, they will think that you are one of the most wonderful people they have ever met!

A young man consulted me about a problem, and in the process of taking his history, he told me that for years he felt he was a social misfit. He was not able to sustain a relationship on a date. Typically, the date started off great but ended up disastrous. He never had a second date with the same woman. He finally decided that he would never be able to get married.

One day, his best friend was drafted to Vietnam and asked a favor of him. "While I'm away, show Lois a good time." He was happy to help his friend, and periodically took Lois to dinner or to a movie. He was not interested in developing a romantic relationship with Lois; he was only doing his friend a favor. Lois fell in love with him, and they are happily married.

What happened was that because he thought of himself as unlikable, he tried to impress his date, and this went over like a lead balloon. When he took out Lois, he was very relaxed. He had no reason to impress her, because he was just meeting her to do his friend a favor. His natural personality was very pleasant when he was not trying to be someone else, and Lois fell in love with him. Operating on manual was self-defeating, but when he could operate on automatic, he was successful.

Are You a Victim of "Internal Terrorism"?

For the past few decades, we have been very conscious and concerned about terrorism. We have tried to adopt a defensive posture, but in contrast to a war with another country, defending ourselves against terrorism is very difficult. We may not know who the enemies are or where they are coming from.

There can also be "internal terrorism" if some force within us makes us do things that are self-destructive. Like external terrorism, we may be unaware of where the enemy is.

One man said, "When I heard of people who had two personalities, I was envious of them. I had about *sixteen* personalities. There were sixteen different voices in my head telling me what to do. Sometimes I would listen to one, at other times to another. I was messing myself up. I went for some therapy, and my psychologist pointed out to me that *I was chairman of the board*. Anyone can say what he wishes, but I don't have to listen to anyone if I don't want to.

"I had never thought of myself as chairman of the board. In fact, I didn't think there *was* a chairman of the board, just a bunch of opinions. If there would be a chairman of the board, it would hardly be me. I didn't have enough self-confidence to occupy that position."

It may seem paradoxical, but the people who are most likely to be self-conscious are those who lack a clear concept of the "self." Or to put it another way, people who have a real "self" are not apt to be self-conscious.

Some people are not at peace with who they are. In fact, they may not even be certain just who they are. They may not trust their own judgment as to who they should be, and they may try to please everyone by conforming to what others want them to be. We all may have different roles in a variety of circumstances, but as long as we consciously decide what we wish to do in each role, we can have a healthy personality. The different roles need not conflict with one another. However, if we alter our personality like a chameleon to adapt to whatever others expect or desire us to be, we really have no personality that we can claim as our own.

We can steer a way through life or drift through it, being carried whichever way the wind blows.

A drifter has no goal. It is difficult to have a sense of self if one has no idea of what one should be and why.

Failure to determine what one wants out of life is often the result of low self-esteem and little confidence in one's ability to make good judgments. Making judgments carries a feeling of responsibility, and a person may feel guilty if his judgment was wrong. The fact is that as long as we do the best we can and are sincere in making judgments, we should not feel guilty if the results are unfavorable. The right or wrong about a judgment should be based on how we arrived at it and not by what resulted.

Suppose that a physician is avaricious and performs unnecessary surgery on a patient for no reason other than to collect a fee. He happens to discover an unsuspected cancer and removes it. He has saved the person's life, but he is an unscrupulous doctor. On the other hand, a doctor may agonize over whether or not to perform a risky operation. He consults other physicians and discusses the options with the family. He finally decides that the operation holds the best chance for preserving the patient's life. Unfortunately, the patient does not survive the surgery. This latter doctor is ethical and trustworthy.

Whom would you choose as your doctor? The first doctor who accidentally happened to save the patient's life is a cheat, whereas the second doctor, whose patient did not survive, is honest.

We are not prophets. We cannot predict results. Our responsibility is to do the best we can.

However, a person with low self-esteem may feel devastated by a failure, regardless of how careful he was in making a judgment. He may, therefore, avoid making judgments and allow others to make decisions for him. If things do not turn out well, it is not his fault.

Dereliction in making judgments lowers one's self-esteem. A person cannot feel good about himself if he allows others to decide things for him. The failure to make judgments further depresses one's self-esteem, resulting in a destructive, vicious cycle.

Without a goal in life, a person may be chronically unsatisfied. One may live just for the gratification of the moment. The prototype of one who seeks such gratification is the drug addict. He may have a very pleasurable "high," but as soon as that passes, he is more miserable than ever.

Most people who seek momentary gratification do not think of themselves as being drug addicts, and there is obviously a difference between someone who uses drugs and a person who drifts through life motivated only by momentary gratification, but in principle they are quite similar. Both are chronically unhappy.

A young man consulted me about a decision. He had completed a year of training in radiology, but he was not pleased with that specialty. He was undecided whether to switch to anesthesiology or pathology. Prior to radiology, he had spent a year in internal medicine, but he was unhappy with that. I asked him whether he had been in any other program prior to medical school, and he said that he was in engineering but hadn't liked that. I suspected that this young man was actually dissatisfied with himself rather than with any particular profession or specialty.

As a child, I used to be lulled to sleep with stories. One story my mother would tell me was amusing, but I did not get its message for many, many years. This young man's problem brought the story to mind.

> *There was once a stonecutter who earned his livelihood by hewing out rocks from the mountain. This was backbreaking work, and he would often bewail his fate. "Why was I destined to be so lowly and humble? Why are some other people so wealthy and mighty, while I break my bones from dawn to dusk to put bread on the table for my family?"*
>
> *One day, as he was engaged in this reverie, he heard a loud tumult in the distance. Climbing to the top of the mountain, he could see a parade from afar. The king was in a royal procession. On either side of the road there were throngs of people shouting, "Bravo!" and throwing flowers at the royal coach.*
>
> *"How wonderful it must be to be so great and powerful," the stonecutter said. "I wish I could be king."*

This happened to be his moment of grace during which his wishes would be granted. He suddenly found himself transformed. He was the king, clad in ermine, sitting in a royal coach drawn by white horses, receiving the acclaim of the crowd. Ah! he thought. How wonderful it is to be the mightiest in all the land.

After a bit, he began to feel very uncomfortable. The bright sun was shining down on him, making him sweat and squirm in his royal robes. "What is this?" he said. "If I am the mightiest in the land, then nothing should be able to affect me. If the sun can humble the king, then the sun is mightier than the king. But I wish to be the mightiest of all! I wish to be the sun."

Immediately, he found himself transformed into the sun. He felt his mighty, unparalleled force of energy. He could give light and warmth to everything in the world. It was his energy that made vegetation grow. If he wished, he could cause devastating fires when angry. "I am indeed the mightiest of all," he said.

But suddenly he found himself very frustrated. He wished to direct his powerful rays at a given point, but was unable to do so. A great cloud had moved beneath him and obstructed his rays. "Here, here!" he said. "If I am the mightiest, then nothing should be able to hinder me. If a cloud can frustrate the sun, then it must be mightier than the sun. I wish to be the mightiest of all. I wish to be a cloud!"

As a great, heavy cloud, he felt very powerful when he dumped torrents of rain wherever he wished, and especially when he blocked the mighty sun. But his joy was short-lived, because suddenly he was swooped away by a sharp gust of wind before which he was helpless.

"Aha," he cried, "so the wind is mightier than a cloud! Then I shall be the wind."

Transformed into a wind, he roared over oceans, churning up immense waves. He blew over forests, toppling tall trees as if they were toothpicks. "Now I am truly the mightiest of all," he said.

But suddenly, he felt himself stymied. He had come up against a tall mountain, and blow as he might, he could not budge it nor get past. "So!" he said. "If a mountain can stop the wind, it is mightier than the wind. Then I wish to be a mountain."

As a tall mountain, he stood majestically, his peak reaching above the clouds. Now he was indeed formidable. Neither the sun nor the wind could affect him. He was the mightiest of all!

All at once he felt a sharp pain. A stonecutter with a sharp pickax was tearing pieces out of him. "How can this be?" he asked. "If someone can dismember me, then he must be even mightier than I am. But I wish to be the mightiest. I wish to be that man." His wish was granted, and he was transformed into the mightiest of all: a stonecutter.

I told this story to the young man. I suggested that he stop switching specialties and get some help in finding himself. Otherwise he might find himself repeatedly making changes and be unhappy with each.

There are people who have changed friends, jobs, locations, religions, and even spouses in the hope of finding comfort. Not only are these changes futile, but they also intensify the problem.

People often see their identity as being dependent on what they do. If they were asked to describe themselves, they might begin with, "I am a lawyer" or "I am a teacher." It is rather unusual for them to say, "I am a caring person. I love people." Or, "I am a person who prefers solitude. Other than with my family, I prefer being left alone. I read and listen to music." Or, "I am a very religious person."

Rather than tell something about themselves, they tell about what they do.

One of the unfortunate consequences of identity by what

one does is that if one is disabled or retires and no longer *does* anything, he or she may lose a feeling of worth. This may significantly contribute to the depression that occurs when people can no longer ply their trade.

Some people seek external identities. They feel that having an impressive home or a luxury car in their driveway gives them an identity.

External identities are fickle. If the impressive house or the luxury automobile constitutes one's identity, then that identity accompanies the house and car when they are sold.

What we do or what we have comprises just a small part of our identity. We should not allow these to be the totality of our identity.

Some people do not have an identity because they have simply not given it any thought. One can go through the motions of living for ninety years without giving any thought to one's identity. But without an identity, one is, as it were, at the mercy of the elements. One gets carried by the wind and is deposited wherever the wind blows rather than where one should belong.

The Problem with a Pseudo-Identity

Earlier, I pointed out the apparent paradox that people who are self-conscious are those who do not have a valid concept of their "self." I came to this discovery the hard way. In fact, I might as well tell you that much of what I have learned about the problems of self-consciousness and a faulty self-image are the result of my personal struggle.

The moment of truth occurred this way. I had become medical director of a huge acute-treatment psychiatric hospital, with an emergency room that served a population of several million. Not only were my days chaotic without any letup, but the nights were equally hectic. On a "good" night I was awoken only six times.

I must preface that I share the problem of chronic low-back pain with millions of other people. Someone recommended that I take the mineral baths at Hot Springs, Arkansas, which were reputed to have restored invalids to complete health. As a scientific physician, I dismissed this as just another folk myth.

When vacation time arrived, I was determined to have absolute rest. No fishing, no activities, no sightseeing, just sitting in a quiet room with the blinds drawn and listening to soft music. I needed to be away from all action, enjoyable as it may be. I rejected all suggestions as being fraught with too much activity, and I decided to go to Hot Springs, where there was nothing to do.

Once I was there, it was only logical to take advantage of the miracle cure. I was ushered into a tiny cubicle and drank several cups of naturally heated water, following which I was immersed in a hot whirlpool. I realized I was in the paradise I had sought. I was beyond the reach of patients, families, doctors, nurses, social workers, lawyers, and probation officers. I could rest undisturbed! Furthermore, I had swirling currents of hot water massaging me. This was truly paradise.

After an incredibly enjoyable five minutes, I arose and said, "Now that was exactly what I needed."

"Where are you going, sir?" the attendant asked.

"I'm going to whatever comes next," I said.

"You can't go on to the next part of the treatment until you've had twenty-five minutes of whirlpool," the attendant said. "That's the rule."

I returned to paradise, only to discover that it had changed. It was no longer enjoyable. After a few minutes, I arose saying, "Look, I've got to get out of here."

"Okay," the attendant said, "but that's it for the treatment."

Not wanting to forfeit the treatment, I returned to the whirlpool for fifteen minutes of pure agony. What had been paradise was now purgatory.

Later that day I realized that I'd had a rude awakening. I was able to take the unrelenting pressure and stress of the hospital for *three years*, but I could not tolerate paradise for more than *eight minutes*. Where had I gone wrong?

After a bit of reflection, things became clear. I had been seeking relaxation, but my concept of relaxation was in error.

Most people relax by occupying themselves with some kind of pastime: reading a book, watching a movie, doing handwork, playing golf, listening to music, or watching a ballgame. These are actually *diversions*, as one's attention is focused on the book, golf ball, or television screen. One's attention is, therefore, diverted from everything — *including oneself*!

In the tiny cubicle, I was deprived of all diversions. There was nothing to read, nothing to look at, no one to talk to, nothing to listen to, and nothing to do. With nothing to divert my attention and nothing else in the environment on which to focus, I was left with only myself as the object of my attention. *I was left alone with myself, with nothing to divert me from myself.*

If you have ever been left alone in a room with someone you despise, you know the feeling. The conclusion is inescapable. I could not tolerate being in my own presence!

I realized that I must have an intense dislike of myself.

On my return home, I consulted a psychologist who confirmed my conclusion. The image I had of myself was of someone who was unlikable.

But what was there about me that made me unlikable? A bit of soul-searching revealed that I had an opinion of myself that was quite disgusting. I had never realized that I thought so poorly of myself. The whirlpool was the first time I had been directly confronted with my "self."

With some help from my psychologist colleague, I came to realize that somewhere along the line, probably in early childhood, I had developed a distorted self-concept. Yes, I had a "self," but it was not a valid "self." For over three decades, I had managed to run away from this "self" in a variety of ways. *I was self-conscious the same way one is conscious of a painful pimple on one's nose.* The "self" I had was an uninviting one.

Some early memories confirmed this. In grade school, when the children were dismissed for recess, they all played games, whereas I used to walk around the playground alone. I desperately wanted to play with the other kids, but I had the fear — nay, the conviction — that if I asked to join them, they would say, "Go away, kid. We don't want you." I have no idea why I felt that way about myself, but I clearly remember the fear of being rejected. My only way of avoiding rejection was to stay away from others.

As I grew older, I was forced to interact with people. Still fearing rejection, I resorted to doing all kinds of favors for people in the hope that this would make me more likable and they would accept me. I became a "people-pleaser." I then realized that my erroneous "self" concept had resulted in a self-consciousness that manifested itself in a variety of ways.

This realization initiated an exhaustive search. *I had to get out of my own way.* But what was there about myself that I thought was so despicable? Over a period of years, I came to realize how I had formed mistaken notions about myself. Eventually, I was able to dispel these misconceptions under which I had been functioning for over *thirty years*!

At the time I made this discovery, I was a practicing psychiatrist. I then realized that I was not alone in having an erroneous self-concept. Many of the people who consulted me because of their emotional problems were in the same boat. Like me, they had a self-image that made them self-conscious. My job was to help them *get out of their own way.*

What happened to me and what happens to so many others is the subject of this book. We need to examine whether we may be "in our own way," and if so, how we can "get out of our own way" so that we can become happier and function better.

How Can I Be in My Own Way?

One of the valuable things I learned from working with alcoholics is that people can be living a blatantly destructive life, ruinous to themselves and their family, be told by everyone that they are self-destructive, yet stubbornly refuse to consider this as a possibility. Delusions may be stronger than reality. If you want to see something in a certain way, nothing will change your mind. In alcoholism, the only thing that may shake someone loose from refusing to recognize reality is a "rock-bottom" phenomenon, something so utterly devastating that it breaks down one's denial.

Whenever we read the following verses in the Torah, I never cease to be amazed. These words were spoken by Moshe Rabbeinu just days before his death:

"See, I have placed before you today the life and the good, and the death and the evil" (*Devarim* 30:15). "I call heaven and earth today to bear witness against you: I have placed life and death before you, blessing and curse, and *you shall choose life*" (ibid., 30:19).

Is it possible that after forty years under Moshe's tutelage, these people have to be told to choose life and blessing rather than death and curse? These were not ignorant, foolish people. They are referred to in Torah literature as the *dor dei'ah*, the generation of knowledge. They were the wisest generation in Jewish history! And yet, these very wise people had to be instructed to choose life and blessing rather than death and curse. It just does not make sense!

Shlomo HaMelech provides the answer. "Each way of a person is right in his own eyes" (*Mishlei* 21:2). But that is not enough. "All the ways of a person are *pure* in his own eyes" (ibid. 16:2). Not only does a person think that his desires are right, he thinks that they are pure, without the least blemish. This misperception is so dangerous that, "If you see a person who is wise in his own eyes, there is more hope for a fool than for him" (ibid. 26:12). Even though a fool lacks wisdom, he does not think he is the wisest person in the world, and may ask someone for advice. Someone who thinks himself very wise is unlikely to ask for advice.

Actually, Shlomo HaMelech is elaborating on the statement in the Torah that forbids a judge from accepting a bribe. "The bribe will blind the eyes of the wise and distort the words of the righteous" (*Devarim* 16:19). Not only does a bribe make one unable to see the truth, but it also distorts one's thinking so that one may see evil as good.

Shlomo spoke from experience. The Torah says that the king should not have many wives because they may mislead him. Shlomo, being the wisest of all men, believed that he would not be influenced by his wives. However, the wisdom of Torah is superior to even the greatest human wisdom. In spite of his great wisdom, Shlomo was influenced by his wives.

The culprit in misleading us is the *yetzer hara*. In order that we should have *bechirah*, Hashem has made the forces of good and the forces of evil equal in strength (*Koheles* 7:14). That is why the Talmud says that the greater a person is, the greater is his *yetzer hara*. That is why Shlomo cautions us, "Do not rely on your own understanding" (*Mishlei* 3:5), and why the Talmud says, "Make someone into your teacher and acquire a friend" (*Pirkei Avos* 1:6). They are not subject to your biases and may see that to which you have been blinded.

Moshe was well aware that even his forty years of teaching may fail to impress people. He said, "It will be when all these things come upon you — the blessing and the curse that I have presented before you — then you will take it to your heart among all the nations where Hashem, your God, has dispersed you, and you will return unto Hashem, your God, and listen to His voice" (*Devarim* 30:1-2). In other words, I know that your refusal to accept My teachings will give way only when your deviance results in a "rock-bottom."

Shlomo HaMelech is right. The obstinacy in refusing to recognize reality stands in one's way to success; "Each way of a person is right in his own eyes."

But what constitutes a convincing "rock-bottom"? Perhaps the following anecdote is demonstrative.

> *Sylvan was the president of a bank in a small town. He was respected as a prominent citizen. Sylvan drank to excess and refused the entreaties of his wife, Phyllis, to seek help for his drinking problem.*
>
> *One day Sylvan woke up to find the house a shambles, as though struck by a tornado. Phyllis and the children were gone. He called his in-laws, and Phyllis was indeed there. "What happened to the house?" he asked.*
>
> *Phyllis said, "You don't remember anything? You were drunk and you went crazy, breaking things."*
>
> *Sylvan did not believe her until his ten-year-old daughter said,*

"I was afraid you were going to kill Mommy."

Sylvan rushed to his in-laws. He wept with bitter remorse, begging Phyllis's forgiveness. "I just couldn't believe the things you were saying about me, but now I know. You will never have to say a single word to me about alcohol. I will never even look at another drop. I will get a repair crew to put the house back in shape."

Phyllis said, "I am not going back into that house with you until you go to an alcohol treatment center."

Sylvan said, "I can't do that. I cannot jeopardize my position at the bank and my reputation in town."

He ran to his minister and confided in him, asking him to intervene. With every good intention, the minister told Phyllis, "Sylvan has come to his senses. He realizes his problem. He promises he will never drink again. Don't break up the family."

Phyllis relented. Sylvan kept his promise for three whole weeks, then drank just a little bit. Before long, he was back to heavy drinking. He could not get out of his own way.

But It's Only an Attitude

An attitude is a "way," and it can be toxic, as pointed out by this chassidic story.

Munisch was a tailor in the Polish town of Moglinitz. It was generally a poor town, and few people could afford custom-made clothes. Munisch's work consisted of matching torn garments or making alterations.

One day, Munisch was surprised to see a handsome coach pull up before his humble shop, and out stepped the local poritz (lord). "Look here, Jew," the poritz said. "I've heard that you do good work. I've brought you some imported fabric, and I want you to sew a garment for me. If you do your work well, you will be well paid."

Munisch bowed to the poritz. "I will do my utmost to please your Lordship. This is a great honor for me." He then took the poritz's measurements and arranged for fittings. When Munisch delivered the finished garment to the castle, the poritz was beside himself with praise. "I have never seen such masterful work before, Jew! You will be the tailor for all my staff." Munisch continued to sew for the poritz, to the latter's great delight.

Munisch was well paid, and he began making significant donations to the shul. He then began making demands for recognition as a major donor, such as being called to the Torah for shlishi, the most dignified aliyah. He also demanded a seat on the easternmost bench, and the first hakafah on Simchas Torah.

One day, the poritz said, "There is going to be an assembly of the area poritzim. Some have their clothes sewn in France, others in Italy. I want to show them garments that will put them all to shame."

When the poritz tried on the new garments, he flew into a rage. He threw the clothes at Munisch. "These are hideous! Do you want to humiliate me in front of my peers? Take these away and bring them back when they are sewn properly, or I'll have you cast into the dungeon."

Munisch left the poritz's castle confused, bewildered, and heartbroken. Where had he gone wrong? He had done his work carefully as always. There was nothing he could do differently. Munisch knew that the poritz was irascible and could make good on his threat to have him thrown into the dungeon. Being at his wits' end, Munisch decided to seek the advice of the Rebbe of Moglinitz.

Munisch broke out in bitter tears, telling the Rebbe his hopeless predicament and asking the Rebbe to save him. The Rebbe said to him, "Munisch, I will tell you what to do, but you must promise to follow my instructions. I want you to take the garments and undo all the seams, then resew the garments exactly along the previous seams."

This made no sense whatsoever to Munisch, but he had emunah that the Rebbe would not mislead him. He carefully and tearfully undid all the seams, then carefully redid them at their former places.

Trembling, he brought the garments to the poritz, who exclaimed, "Munisch, this is the most beautiful work you have ever done. Those poritzim will realize that their French and Italian tailors can't hold a candle to my Munisch."

Munisch returned to the Rebbe, grateful but bewildered. "The garments were exactly the same as before," he told the Rebbe.

The Rebbe said, "Munisch, there is more that goes into the work of an artisan than just his dexterity. His feelings and attitudes imbue themselves as well and give flavor to it. As long as you were the humble Munisch, your anivus invested itself in your work. Anivus is a beautiful trait, and it gave chein to the garment. But when you became a baal ga'avah, the ugliness of the ga'avah went into the garment. No wonder the poritz rejected it.

"When you resewed the garment, you were brokenhearted. Your ga'avah was gone, and your anivus returned, which gave the same garment its charm."

It is important to remember that whether it is a service one provides or an item one fashions, there is more to it than is visible to the eye. Our attitudes can get in our way and convert success to failure.

I Had to Get My Head Outta My Way

This man's story was one of the most important lessons of my life. He related this story in his fortieth year of sobriety. He was the leading trial lawyer in Pittsburgh.

"Early in my law career," he said, "my boss told me that I was an alcoholic, and that if I wanted to keep my job, I must attend AA meetings. Although I thoroughly disagreed with him, I did not want to lose my job. I attended the meetings fairly regularly but kept on drinking.

"After a while, I said to one of the veteran members, 'Why isn't this program working for me? I attend the meetings, but I still drink.'

"The old timer said to me, 'Young fella, I've been watching you. You're trying to understand how this program works. Stop it. Just listen and do as you're told. Don't try to figure out why.'

"I was deeply offended. 'What do you think I am, some kind of idiot? I am an intelligent lawyer, and I have to think through everything I do. I can't just "do as you're told without understanding why."'

"As time went on, I came to realize that as an intelligent lawyer, I was getting drunk. This old-timer must be doing something right. So I decided to try it his way, and here I am today, forty years sober.

"It's obvious that my thinking was working against me."

I subsequently found that this is also true in matters of *emunah*. If we try to reason things out, our minds may get in our way.

God is infinite. Our minds have never had any experience with anything infinite. We may have many questions about God, but when we try to understand anything about Him, we end up totally confused and frustrated. It is much like being told that the temperature in the room is seventy-five degrees, and you want to make sure for yourself that this is true, but the only measuring instrument is a watch. It happens to be a very good watch and accurately measures time, but it is of no use measuring temperature. If you insist on trying to measure temperature with a watch, you will be confused and frustrated.

Rambam was an accomplished philosopher as well as a Talmudic scholar. When he addresses the conflict of God's foreknowledge and man's freedom of choice, he says that this conflict cannot be resolved because we have no idea what God's knowledge is like — hence, we can make no statements about it. This is equally true of everything about God.

All we can do is do like my friend who was unsuccessful when he tried to understand how the recovery program works, but was successful when did as he was told. There are some things that God chose to reveal to us through Moshe and the prophets, but beyond that, trying to understand Infinite God with the limited human mind will get one going around in circles.

For example, by definition, God is absolute perfection, hence He lacks nothing. God cannot desire things the way humans desire, because human desire indicates a lack of something, and if we try to understand His desire according to the nature of human desire, we will be no wiser, and our minds will get in our way.

Why the Negative Self-Concept?

Earlier, I said that I came to realize that somewhere along the line, probably in early childhood, I had developed a distorted self-concept. But even a thorough search failed to reveal what could have caused me to feel this way about myself. My parents were loving and caring. My father's method of discipline was to enhance rather than to depress my self-esteem. If I did something of which he disapproved, he would say in Yiddish, "*Es past nisht*" (that doesn't become you), or in other words, "You're too good for that. Why are you doing something beneath your dignity?" Even his reprimands were delivered in a manner to avoid depressing my self-esteem.

I succeeded at everything I did. I graduated high school at sixteen, received *semichah* at twenty-one, graduated medical school with high honors at twenty-nine, and served as assistant rabbi during medical school. I was board-certified in psychiatry and wrote a number of books. There was no logical reason for me to feel negative about myself, yet I felt that people would not like me unless I did something for them, so I became the world's greatest people-pleaser. I was totally dependent on what others thought of me. If people did not say that my sermon was outstanding, I was devastated. I had no identity. I was whatever you wanted me to be. My achievements did not alleviate my delusion that I was inadequate, undesirable, damaged material. I wrote a book, *Life's Too Short*, in which I described some of the maneuvers that a person may do to relieve the feelings of inadequacy and unworthiness. It is essentially autobiographical.

In my practice of psychiatry, I found the same problem to be operative in most people with emotional disorders. Some blamed their parents, which may have been justified in some, but not in all, cases. I was puzzled by the ubiquity of unwarranted feelings of inferiority. I used many of the maneuvers described in *Life's Too Short*, which provided only transient relief.

Furthermore, there is a phenomenon that appeared inexplicable to me, and that is the "paradox of low self-esteem." I found that gifted and highly intelligent people often had more profound feelings of low self-esteem than people who were less endowed. This made no sense at all.

And so I struggled through decades of adult life, practicing psychiatry and writing books, achieving much recognition, yet unable to shake off the tormenting feeling that I was not good enough.

Several years ago, I was fortunate to come across a comment by Rav Simcha Zissel Ziv of Kelm on the verse in *Tehillim* (118:13), "*Dacho dichisani linpol, vaHashem azarani* — They pushed me hard that I might fall, but Hashem assisted me." Rav Simcha Zissel calls our attention to the apparent duplication of the verb *dacho dichisani*, and makes this amazing comment: "*Dacho* is a noun, not a verb. It refers to the innate depressive force within a person that constantly depresses him to crush him" (*Da'as Chachmah U'Mussar*, Vol. 3, p. 113).

This helps us understand the Talmudic statement, "A person's *yetzer hara* renews itself every day and seeks to destroy him" (*Kiddushin* 30b). The goal of the *yetzer hara* is to make a person nonfunctional, and it achieves this by making him see himself as inferior, inadequate, and unworthy. If the *yetzer hara* tempts a Torah-observant Jew to eat *treif* or violate Shabbos, it knows it is unlikely to succeed because the person knows it is forbidden. However, if it tells the person, "You are a failure. You cannot succeed. You are unlikable. You are damaged goods," the person does not recognize that this is the wile of the *yetzer hara*, and he may be defenseless.

Of course, negative influences, such as parental neglect or abuse or illness, intensify the feelings of inferiority, but even in absence of such factors, a person can have low self-esteem. The *yetzer hara* has great powers and can delude a person to feel unworthy.

I breathed a sigh of relief. My negative feelings about myself are the result of the *yetzer hara's* efforts to disable me. This is the same *yetzer hara* that tempts a person to commit sins. Just as I can reject the *yetzer hara's* pressure to eat something nonkosher or to do a forbidden act on Shabbos, I can reject its efforts to crush me by making me feel inadequate and unworthy.

Rav Simcha Zissel's insight also explains the "self-esteem paradox." The Talmud says, "The greater a person is, the greater is his *yetzer hara*." This stands to reason. If a person is poorly endowed, Hashem does not give him an overwhelming *yetzer hara*. A person who has greater knowledge and more personality assets may be given a more powerful *yetzer hara* commensurate with his abilities, hence he faces a greater struggle in resisting the *yetzer hara's* attempts to crush him.

When I was president of the Allegheny Medical Society, I arranged for a talk by an out-of-town speaker who was an authority on this particular condition and had written the leading text on it. I watched him lecture to the physicians, and it was clear to me that he was studying the faces in the audience to see if anyone disagreed with him. I thought, *Why do you care if anyone disagrees with you? If they do, they're wrong! You wrote the book on this condition.*

Afterward, I drove the doctor to the airport and waited with him until boarding. His expertise on the subject notwithstanding, his self-esteem was very low, and, irrational as it may be, he was extremely sensitive to someone disagreeing with him.

The person who is in fact bright, personable, worthy, and suffers from unwarranted feelings of negativity is essentially believing a delusion. The *yetzer hara* has extraordinary powers to delude and even cause people to hallucinate. Logic is no match for delusions. (The best advice I was given by a colleague in psychiatric training was from a fellow resident in a discussion about a certain patient. He said, "Twerski, stop talking logic!")

The low self-esteem delusion is the mirror image of the grandiose delusion of a psychotic. One inmate at the Mayview State Hospital in Pennsylvania had been a patient for over twenty years. He had the delusion that he was chief of the World Bank, and the fact that he slept on a cot in a room with forty other patients did not affect his grandiose delusion.

One client, who was a civic leader and who suffered from low self-esteem, said, "I have an entire wall in my home covered with honorary plaques and tributes from civic organizations. They mean nothing to me." When he received an accolade, he felt better about himself for a very brief period, and then the low self-esteem delusion recurred.

I believe that the self-esteem problem is most often the work of the *yetzer hara*, who seeks to disable a person. Unless one realizes that this is the yetzer hara at work, one may not escape this destructive delusion.

The Burnout Phenomenon

Working for *parnasah* is an essential of life. It is not unusual for people who were satisfied with their jobs to become bored and feel that they are "burned out." Here are some examples.

An accountant, after more than twenty years of successful practice: "I can't live a life of adding and subtracting figures all day. When I take out the books from my desk drawers in the morning, they feel like they weigh a ton."

A pediatrician: "More kids with runny noses and persistent cough. A mother comes in with two kids, complaining of being exhausted by their constant bickering and whining. Lady, what do you want from me? I don't know how much longer I can take this daily grind."

A lawyer: "I've got to move on to something else. I'm a partner in a major law firm and I'm making more money than I ever dreamed of. I'm going to leave the firm. I don't know just what I'm going to do, but I'm bored to death."

A nurse: "I'm sicker than all of the patients in the hospital. I'm sick of guilt-ridden family members who criticize the care we give the patient. I'm sick of ego-crazed doctors who think they're God. I'm sick of patients who smoke and drink themselves to death and insist we cure them. There must be other ways to make a living."

An appliance store salesperson: "This job is not for me anymore. People come in and want to know every detail about an appliance. They take my time and energy, then go and buy the appliance elsewhere for twenty dollars less. Eighteen years of this is enough."

Millions of people are staying in jobs they hate just to keep their health insurance. Some polls have shown that relatively few people are really satisfied with their job.

The list is endless. The common denominator is that people who for years were satisfied with what they were doing develop progressive dissatisfaction. Many of them make changes that are often most unwise — change jobs and lose seniority; move to another neighborhood and lose old friendships; divorce and lose the person who loved them the most — all for what? Because of *burnout*.

The workplace is not the only site for burnout. Many instances of "midlife crisis" are burnout phenomena.

A husband: "I don't know what happened that the excitement of our marriage fizzled. I thought that when the first grandchild came along that would rejuvenate us, but it hasn't. My life at home is too humdrum."

A college student: "It's a drag to get to school every day. It used to be exciting, but it's terribly boring now. The only good thing about college is the frat."

Yes, the colloquial term for these phenomena is "burnout." Boredom with one's job or loss of enthusiasm in a relationship is common. Employers try various tactics to prevent a veteran employee from leaving because he is "burned-out," and marriage counselors try to investigate why a relationship that was rich in love deteriorated. Sometimes these measures are indeed effective, but at other times they do not resolve the problem completely, if at all.

There are undoubtedly many reasons for burnout. Having one difficult-to-please boss is stressful enough. Having *two* difficult-to-please bosses who don't see eye-to-eye and have different and even conflicting demands is much worse. Being assigned responsibility without authority or means to get it done is most stressful. Yet these in themselves are not really burnout. They are simply impossible situations. Such situations may indeed be resolved by making it clear to management that they are asking for the impossible and working with them to make the assignment possible. If this does not succeed, there may be no alternative to changing jobs.

Changes in industry, commerce, and manufacturing can make a person's job difficult, if not intolerable. There is excellent advice in books on the subject, such as *Toxic Work,* by Barbara Bailey Reinhold.

It is also possible for a person to be a misfit. My personal experience was that I had hoped to be the kind of rabbi my father was, a counselor who helped people with sundry problems. My first pulpit was in 1952. After World War II, psychology and psychiatry had a meteoric rise, and after three years as a rabbi, I realized that people would not consult me as they did my father, because the mantle of counseling had gone over to the mental health professional. My job would essentially be performing rituals and ceremonies, which was not to my taste. I was disillusioned, and I switched careers to become a psychiatrist so that I could do what I had hoped to do as a rabbi. We are sometimes disappointed when the job we have fails to live up to expectations. This is *not* what I refer to as burnout.

By "burnout" I am referring to a situation where a person

who was quite satisfied with work or with a relationship for an extended period of time loses interest and becomes dissatisfied. "Burned-out" is a good descriptive term for this condition, and the better we understand the phenomenon, the better we may be able to avoid it or apply corrective measures more effectively.

There is another not uncommon condition that may properly be termed burnout. A person is coasting along at sixty miles an hour and comes to a very steep hill. He shifts into a gear that can give him the necessary power to navigate the hill. Once he reaches the top of the hill and is again on level terrain, he shifts back into the "drive" gear and travels smoothly at sixty miles an hour.

But suppose that upon reaching the top of the hill, he finds his gear is stuck and he cannot shift into "drive." The gear that is suited for ascending a steep hill cannot go beyond thirty-five miles an hour. He is not going to be able to reach his destination until much later than he had planned. Furthermore, this gear, although more powerful, is intended for short spurts. If he drives several hundred miles in this gear, the gear may "burn out."

This has its parallel in life. In developing a career, a person may have to be aggressive. For example, if one wishes to enter medical school, one may find there is stiff competition, and in order to beat others out in the admission process, one may have to exert extra energy — because the difference between a 3.6 grade point average and a 3.7 grade point average may determine one's entire life. In business, too, the competition is fierce, and a person may have to push with both elbows to succeed.

However, one may reach a stage where this degree of aggressiveness and competitiveness is no longer necessary.

One can "coast," as it were. However, having been in an aggressive mode, one may not be able to "shift gears," and one may exert oneself even though it is no longer necessary. Like driving long distances in the more powerful gear, one may burn out.

We need to know how to use our energies appropriately and not fall into a pattern of behavior that was appropriate for one stage of life but is no longer appropriate.

The following incident helped me understand burnout. On returning from yeshivah, my son told me about his resourceful roommate. Because of fire hazard, the boys were not permitted to have electrical appliances in the dormitory rooms. However, because the boys did their own laundry, they were permitted to have a clothes iron. What the roommate did was turn the iron upside down, wedge the handle in a closed drawer, and eureka! He had a hot surface on which he could make coffee, popcorn, or toast. What ingenuity!

But then, why do we need a number of different heat-producing appliances? Why not just use the clothes iron?

The heat of the clothes iron is produced by a delicate metal filament, which turns red-hot when an electric current is passed through it. If the iron is used only for what it was intended, it has a normal life expectancy. If, however, in addition to ironing clothes, it is also used as a coffee maker, toaster, popcorn maker, and griddle, the filament will burn out in a relatively short period of time. Why? Because it was not designed to carry the extra load of providing so many hours of heat. The delicate filament can't take it and will soon burn out.

That is very often the reason for burnout. Everything in life has a purpose, and when used for the purpose for which it was designed, it has a normal life expectancy. However, if you have unrealistic expectations of anything, making excessive demands of it and placing a greater burden on it than it was meant to carry, it will, like the element in the clothes iron, simply burn out.

Here's an example. Let's assume that the purpose of an automobile is to provide transportation. You've had a car for six years and you have maintained it according to the manufacturer's instructions. Although it has over one hundred thousand miles, it is still in excellent shape and runs smoothly. The few scratches and the minor dents on the bumper are insignificant. It can still serve you well for several more years. There really is no reason to trade it in and assume a major expenditure for a new model.

But what if you want the car to do more than provide transportation? Suppose it is an ego thing. Several of your neighbors have new cars, and if you have this old model in your driveway, what does that say about you? That you're not as successful as they are. The car, then, is more than a vehicle for transportation. It is a status symbol. While it is still a very efficient vehicle, it is of no value as a status symbol. In other words, as a status symbol, it has burned out. If you have need of a status symbol, you may assume a large debt to buy a new car. The life expectancy of a well-maintained vehicle may be ten years, but the life expectancy of a status symbol may be only three years, after which it is "burned out." A person may have six transportation vehicles during a lifetime, but may have eighteen or more status-symbol vehicles during a lifetime.

The human body requires adequate nutritional input for optimal function. The human psyche, too, requires adequate emotional nutrition for its optimal function. Deprivation of emotional input can have negative consequences on a person's emotional and even physical health. For example, the classic study by Renee Spitz showed that infants who were not adequately cuddled in the first six months of life failed to thrive and had severe depression. At any phase of life, there is an amount of emotional input necessary for emotional health.

Nutritionists tell us that for optimum health, one must have a balanced diet. A diet top-heavy in only one type of food may provide the requisite number of calories, but does not provide the essential elements that the body requires.

This is also true of emotional "nutrients." There are various sources of emotional input: family, friends, work, literature, art, music, hobbies, religion, etc. These combine, in amounts that vary, to equal the 100 percent of emotional input each person requires. For example, one person may receive the 100 percent emotional input from:

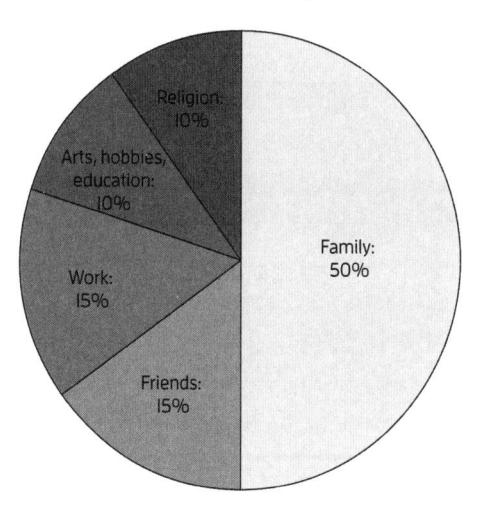

- Family: 50%
- Friends: 15%
- Work: 15%
- Arts, hobbies, education: 10%
- Religion: 10%

Another person may receive the 100 percent emotional input from:

Education:
5%

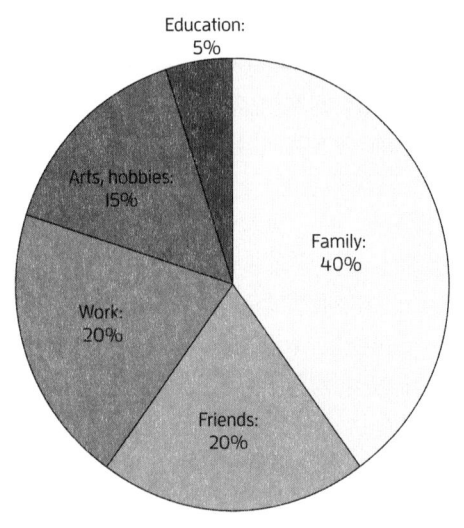

Arts, hobbies:
15%

Family:
40%

Work:
20%

Friends:
20%

In both cases, the lion's share of emotional input derives from meaningful interpersonal relationships and non-work-related sources. This is as it should be. Although these figures are not etched in stone, the optimum balance requires a major input from sources other than work

This thesis is confirmed by the work of Boston psychologist Rosalind Barnett, who found that both men and women in good relationships were able to withstand workplace stress better than people who tried to deal with difficult work situations without that support.[1] Barbara B. Reinhold reports the finding that 89 percent of working mothers reported that their parenting experiences made them more effective at work.[2]

Work is primarily to provide one with a livelihood. There is also an emotional component in work when one takes pride in one's accomplishments and productivity. Generally, work should provide a relatively smaller proportion of the

---

[1] R. Barnett, "Home-to-Work Spillover Revisited: A Study of Full-time Employed Women in Dual-Earner Couples," *Journal of Marriage and Family* 56 (3) (1994): 647-56.

[2] B. Reinhold, *Toxic Work* (New York: Plume-Penguin Books, 1997).

100 percent requirement.

Suppose that a person has few, if any, family ties. He may have no family or may be detached from his family. He may have few close friends. His interest in religion and the humanities is limited.

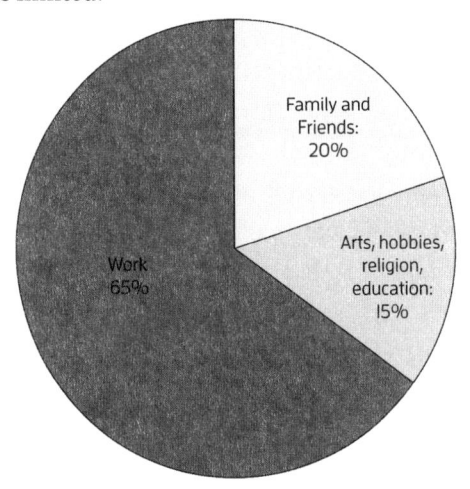

Pie chart: Work 65%; Family and Friends: 20%; Arts, hobbies, religion, education: 15%

This person has an inordinate expectation of work, i.e., that in addition to providing a livelihood, it should provide the lion's share of his emotional needs. But work is not designed to do that, and calling upon work to do so much is like expecting the filament in the iron to provide heat for a toaster, corn popper, coffee maker, and griddle. Like the filament, the work is likely to burn out. It cannot carry the extra load.

True, accommodations at the workplace may be made so that it is capable of producing, say, 35 percent of the total input required, but it is unlikely that it can realistically provide 65 percent of the total. This demand of the workplace is much greater than it can realistically provide. This person can become very unhappy, with any of a variety of symptoms of discontent.

Sometimes the person blames the particular work situation and changes jobs. The novelty of a new job may give some relief, but, obviously, this job is not capable of producing the amount of emotional input he needs any more than did the previous job, and his dissatisfaction is likely to recur.

Burnout can cause a person to be depressed, irritable, and angry. In may result in loss of interest, not only in work, but in other areas as well. It may result in insomnia and can contribute to a variety of medical disorders. If this person seeks to get relief from alcohol or drugs, he is vulnerable to becoming addicted. He may look for the thrills of gambling or forbidden relationships. He may not attribute his unhappiness to burnout and may instead find fault with his wife, leading to marital difficulties and possibly divorce.

Case #1

Jennifer was a secretary in a busy law firm. Her job was exciting. She got to meet many people, and there was never a dearth of interesting cases. She was happily married, or at least she thought she was. She had one daughter, age ten. She enjoyed caring for the family. Her mother lived nearby, and she saw her quite often.

Jennifer's husband, Norbert, was a manufacturer's representative, and he often made out-of-town trips. One day, Jennifer opened a letter from Norbert's firm, and it said that for cost-containment purposes, no personal calls could be made on the office line. Attached was a list of personals calls Norbert had made in the past two months, 90 percent of them to one number. Jennifer asked Norbert to whom these calls were made, and after hemming and hawing, he admitted that he was involved in a forbidden relationship.

In spite of marriage counseling and pastoral counseling, the marriage broke up. Just about this time, Jennifer's mother died.

Jennifer was understandably depressed by these losses, and she sought psychotherapy. She threw herself more into her job, but gradually became dissatisfied at work. Whereas she'd previously had very pleasant relations with everyone in the office, she became withdrawn and hypercritical.

The breakup of her marriage and her mother's death were certainly adequate reasons for Jennifer's emotional changes. However, her attempt to compensate for the emotional vacuum resulting from these losses by expecting more from her work was unrealistic. There had been no change in the workplace to account for Jennifer's dissatisfaction with work. The work "filament" had burned out.

Downsizing, outsourcing, and other changes in the economy are certainly capable of producing much stress, but *stress is not the same as burnout*. How one reacts to stress will determine its effects, and burnout sharply curtails optimal reactions to stress.

Case #2

At forty-four, Jerome was a mid-level manager in a financial firm he had been with for sixteen years. As rumors spread about a possible merger, Jerome felt insecure about his job. His wife, Elaine, reassured him that even if his position were eliminated, they would find a way to survive.

Two years later, Jerome's anxieties materialized. He was carrying a load of supporting two children in college. He felt that the chances of finding a new job in his field at age forty-six were slim. With Elaine's encouragement, Jerome interviewed with several financial advisers, and eventually was hired, albeit at a lesser salary than he'd had at the first firm.

Both children took part-time jobs, and Elaine managed the household budget efficiently. In spite of the blow to his self-esteem by taking a lesser-paying job, Jerome felt understood and appreciated by his family. He did *not* experience burnout.

To avoid the risk of experiencing burnout, with any of its many destructive consequences, a person should seek to establish healthy family ties and broaden one's interests. It is not unusual for a person to become so engrossed in his work that almost nothing else exists for him. He may neglect attending family events, and even his relationship with his wife and children, let alone with extended family members, may be distant. He may not allow himself time for reading anything but work-related material, and he is simply too busy to cultivate a hobby.

I don't underestimate the importance of one's work, but one really shouldn't call the office multiple times when on vacation. *Working to live is okay; living to work is not.* One should leave word with the secretary to call only in case of an emergency and then enjoy the vacation with the family.

Make time for interests and activities other than work. "But," you may say, "I just don't have the luxury of such time." Sure you do. You just don't know it.

A man entered a motel that had a prominent "No Vacancy" sign and asked for a room. The clerk pointed out that they were entirely full.

"Don't tell me that," the man said. "You mean if the president of the United States came, you wouldn't find a room for him?"

"Well," the clerk said, "if the president came, we'd have to make room for him."

"Good," the man said, "the president isn't coming. You can give me his room."

Regardless of how busy one's schedule is, if a serious emergency arose, one would find time to attend to it. Realize that strengthening relationships and broadening your interests are every bit as important as attending to a serious emergency. Make time for these, and you may avoid costly burnout.

Will the Real Self Please Stand Up?

Many problems ascribed to "selfishness" are due to a misunderstanding of what the "self" is.

The human being is a composite creature, comprised of a physical body and "something else." Science classifies man as *homo sapiens*, which in plain English means "a hominoid (baboon, gorilla) with intellect." Man is just another variety of animal. We understand, however, that man is more than an intelligent gorilla.

Every living creature is endowed with the means to fulfill itself. The human being has some features animals lack, and it is this that gives him his uniqueness. Foremost among these features is the ability to conceptualize a purpose for his existence. Bees are endowed with the unique engineering skill to make perfect hexagonal structures, and beavers are endowed with the skill to build efficient dams. These are innate abilities. Although we have no way of knowing what bees and beavers think or whether they think at all, I doubt that bees think, "My job is to make hexagonal honeycombs. I must concentrate on making the most precise hexagons." If they did, they might experiment with making honeycombs of different shapes, which no bee has ever done.

God created man with an animal-type body and then "blew into his nostrils the soul of life" (*Bereishis* 2:7), which we conveniently refer to as the "human spirit." It is this spirit that enables us to contemplate a purpose in life. Another crucial feature of the spirit is that it enables a person to make choices of what he wants to do. Animals are not free to make choices. They must do what their body desires. Hence, animals are not free. Humans, by virtue of *bechirah*, can defy a bodily desire. It is this *bechirah* that enables man to live by morals and ethics, which animals cannot do, and which defines him as human.

The *Zohar* capitalizes on the verse that God "blew into his nostrils the soul of life," saying that this metaphor means that the "soul of life" is essentially Godly. "One who exhales expresses something from within oneself." Inasmuch as God is absolute and indivisible, it follows that, in spirit, all humans are one. The fact that we are all individuals is due to the fact that our physical bodies have boundaries that set us apart. Hence, the *Tanya* says, the more we emphasize our physical component, the more we are separate. The more we emphasize our spirit, the more we are united.

When we refer to someone as being "selfish," we mean that he is satisfying a bodily want, and if doing so encroaches on another person's comfort, the term is pejorative. Philosophically, he is not really being selfish any more than having his automobile engine lubricated is selfish. The body is the vehicle through which the "self," the spirit, functions.

What is "my way," my purpose in life? It is not satisfying the body, the physical component. My real self is the spirit, and I must keep the body in optimal condition because it is the vehicle via which the spirit functions. But the body's demands often get in the way of the spirit, and it poses obstacles to the spirit. In order to allow the spirit, the real "me," to reach its goal and achieve its purpose, I must bring the body under the control of the spirit. When I do so, I am "getting outta my way."

The problem is that we are easily deluded, and we do not realize that when we yield to the body's desires, we are actually frustrating the real self. This is what happens in addiction. A particular act, be it drinking alcohol, taking drugs, gambling, or lusting, is experienced as a pleasure, and we wish to repeat the sensation. We do not realize that we are not gratifying the real self at all, only the "pseudo-self." Eventually, yielding to the "pseudo-self" results in misery, and when the discomfort resulting from the addiction is greater than the pleasure provided by the addiction, one is ready for recovery. This is referred to as reaching "rock bottom." The addict then realizes that the addiction was really self-defeating, standing in the way of a true self-fulfillment, and that he must "get outta my way."

"Getting outta my way" essentially means giving priority to the spirit, which is the true self. The 12-step programs of Alcoholics Anonymous, Narcotics Anonymous, Gamblers Anonymous, and other 12-step programs provide the framework for a reorientation, and the fellowship provides the support that enables a person to make this character overhaul.

The Pitfall of Extremes

Rambam advocates "The Golden Path" or "The Mean of Virtue" as the ideal path in life, and cautions us to avoid extremes.

Man appears to be subject to extremes. Man's name, "Adam," expresses the two poles of which man is capable: (1) *adamah*, the earth of which man is constituted and which is not conducive to spiritual aspirations, and (2) *adameh*, to resemble. Man was created "in the likeness of God" (*Bereishis* 1:26). Exercising either pole to the extreme can be a serious obstacle to success. If one is not cautious in living within the proper confines of his "likeness to God," he cannot be successful, because man is capable of only a *likeness* to God, not an *identity* with God.

Again, this pitfall is very obvious in the alcoholic, whose refusal to recognize the incontrovertible evidence that he cannot control alcohol is strongly suggestive of a delusion of omnipotence. This trait is also found among nonalcoholics who refuse to accept some limitations.

At an AA meeting in Jerusalem, one attendee related the following story:

> "I first came to this program eight years ago. When I heard that the program required surrendering to a Higher Power, I turned around and left. I don't believe in God. I am an atheist and I won't

work a program that involves God.

"I returned a year later because my wife threw me out of the house. I realized that I needed your help desperately. I said to you, 'I'll do everything you ask of me, just don't pressure me about God,' and you agreed.' After a bit, you said that I had to get a sponsor.

"My sponsor said to me, 'You have to pray every day.' I said, 'Wait a minute. We have an agreement that you won't bother me about God.' My sponsor said, 'So don't pray to God. Just pray.' I said that this doesn't make any sense. What do you mean, 'Pray, but not to God?'

"My sponsor said, 'Look, you asked me to help you, and I'll be glad to, but if you want my help to stay sober, you have to pray every day. If you don't want it, you can stay drunk.'

"I didn't have a choice. There was no way I could stay sober without this program. Today, I'm six years sober. I pray every day, but I don't believe in God. When I pray, it makes me aware that I'm not God."

This man couldn't stop drinking because he had some kind of feeling of omnipotence. The alcoholic cannot admit that he is powerless over alcohol because he cannot accept that he is powerless — he has this delusion that he is Godlike and cannot be powerless.

Alcoholics are not the only people who have delusions of omnipotence. There are many people who have serious life problems because they can't accept that there are ways in which they are powerless. If you can't accept that you're powerless over some things, that notion will stand in your way, and you've got to get out of your own way.

The delusion of omnipotence is often accompanied by a delusion of infallibility. No human being can be perfect. Mistakes are certainly regrettable, but all we can do is recognize them and try to see what caused them so that repetitious mistakes can be avoided. If one cannot accept one's fallibility, one can be paralyzed by guilt.

Getting Out of God's Way

Just as we must get out of our own way, we must get out of God's way, too.

I achieved an insight from one of my patients, a severe alcoholic and drug addict who had achieved excellent sobriety. He said, "Doctor, my recovery is a miracle. There is no way I could have done this. I know that God did this. I just had to get out of His way."

Yes, Hashem does things for us, but sometimes we stand in His way and erect barriers that prevent His mercy from reaching us.

Maharal cites the midrash that even if all the festivals will fall away, Purim will always survive, because *Megillas Esther* says, "These days of Purim will never cease among the Jews." (The Torah commentaries struggle with this midrash. How is it possible that festivals decreed by the Torah will fall away?) Rabi Elazar says, "Yom Kippur, too, will survive" (*Esther* 9:28; *Yalkut Shimoni, Mishlei* 944).

Maharal draws an analogy between Purim and Yom Kippur. (Interestingly enough, the Hebrew "Yom Kippurim" can be read as *yom ki-purim*, which means "a day like Purim.") On Purim, the Jewish people were threatened with annihilation, and their salvation was from death to life. So, too, with Yom Kippur. If the person realizes that sin is a spiritual death, he makes a sincere dedication to avoid sin and live. Just as Hashem wrought a miracle and saved the Jews from annihilation, Hashem can forgive one's sins and restore a person to spiritual life (*Tiferes Yisrael* 53).

What can a person do to eliminate the barriers that obstruct Hashem's help? There is a simple, albeit difficult, solution. Develop *anivus*.

"A person who develops *anivus* can be saved from all sin" (*Yaaros Devash* 1:15).

When the Temple existed, a person who brought an *Olah* offering was rewarded for the *Olah*, and a person who brought a *Minchah* offering was rewarded for a *Minchah*. But if a person has *anivus*, the Torah considers it as if he brought *all* the offerings, as the Psalmist says, 'The sacrifices of God are a broken spirit' (*Tehillim* 51:19; *Sotah* 5b).

A "broken spirit" does not mean depression. Rather, broken spirit means that one has broken his *ga'avah*. *Ga'avah* is the major barrier between man and Hashem. Whereas Hashem's presence is with a person even when one is in a state of contamination (*Vaykira* 16:16), Hashem does not tolerate *ga'avah*. "One with haughty eyes and an expansive heart, him I cannot bear" (*Tehillim* 101:5).

In the introductory *tefillah* of Rebbe Elimelech of Lizhensk, we ask that Hashem eliminate the barriers that separate us from Him. Actually, *we* should remove the barriers, which are primarily the ego. Referring to the giving of the Torah at Sinai, Moshe Rabbeinu said, "I stood between Hashem and you" (*Devarim* 5:5). A more precise translation is, "I *stand* between Hashem and you." Rebbe Yechiel Michel of Zlotchov commented, "It is the *anochi*, the ego, that stands between us and Hashem.

As I pointed out in my writings, one should have a healthy self-esteem, which means that one should be aware of one's potential and have the confidence that he can actualize it. Self-esteem leads to achievement, whereas unwarranted feelings of inadequacy and unworthiness lead to inaction and resignation.

Our great Torah personalities were aware of their abilities, and this enabled them to produce great Torah works and exercise leadership. Nevertheless, they were profoundly humble, and their greatness did not cause them to feel superior to others. Indeed, if a person is aware of his potential and the awesome responsibility he has to fulfill his mission on earth, he is humbled, and this is *anivus*.

Rav Yisrael of Salant said, "I know that my mind is equal to a thousand other minds. By the same token, my responsibilities are a thousandfold as great." His awareness of his greatness was cause for even more *anivus*.

Yes, as we say the *Vidui* on Yom Kippur and reflect on our sins, we should indeed have a broken spirit, a feeling of sadness and contrition. However, this is a broken spirit that can be repaired, and together with the broken spirit we should feel the joy of forgiveness and that we not only have the opportunity to correct our mistakes, but even to elevate ourselves to new spiritual heights.

If we develop *anivus*, Yom Kippur will cleanse us of our sins. Hashem desires to forgive us. We just shouldn't stand in His way.

It's Hard to Believe

The recovery program I was in required that I make a "fearless moral inventory," which took about three years, and that is when I discovered many of my character defects that I am describing. In retrospect, until I was compelled to acknowledge these, I thought I was faultless. It's hard to believe that a person can be so grossly defective yet think oneself to be perfect. But many things can go wrong in our daily lives, at home, at work, and socially. If we think of ourselves as being without fault, then someone else must be responsible for what has gone wrong, and it is not difficult to make a case for blaming someone.

I have written several books interpreting the cartoons of the insightful cartoonist, the late Charles Schulz. One of his characters, Peppermint Patty, is lazy and refuses to study. One day she calls Charlie Brown and says, "I've failed again, Charlie Brown, and it's your fault."

"How can it be my fault?" Charlie asks.

"You're my friend, aren't you?" Patty says. "You should have been a better influence on me."

This kind of reasoning is not uncommon.

Our minds are genius at generating ideas that will satisfy our needs; we are easily biased, and once an opinion takes hold, it may be extremely difficult to dislodge. The *mussar* authorities cite the halachah that a judge may not hear the argument of a litigant in the absence of his opponent. Even though he knows there is an opposing litigant whose opinion he must hear, nevertheless, if he has already been impressed by one opinion, he cannot be objective to the other side. Once we have placed blame for something on someone, it is very difficult to release ourselves from that opinion. In fact, we are likely to build up support for that opinion.

We frequently feel offended or injured, and as a result we feel resentment toward those who offended us. We are taught that we should forgive those who offended us. This is indeed a noble thing to do, but most difficult when the hurt has been deep and severe. One recovering alcoholic was dealt a very harsh blow by some unethical businessmen. I met him one day and he said, "I am very bitter toward those people who took advantage of me and left me penniless. But I will go to an AA meeting tonight and try to divest myself of these resentments, because if I hang on to them, I'll drink again."

I was curious to see how an AA meeting would eliminate his resentments, so I accompanied this man to the AA meeting. He shared his feelings with some peers, who listened empathically. One man with many years of recovery said, "It's tough to forgive a severe hurt, but it's simply stupid to hang on to resentments. Those people couldn't care less how you feel about them. You are the one who will suffer from these hateful feelings. They will ruin your sleep and eat away at your guts. The way I see it, hanging on to resentments is like swallowing poison and expecting the other person to die."

I can't think of any psychotherapy that could have been more helpful.

Noble character traits tend to cluster together. This man

had suffered a severe financial loss. Thirteen years later I received a letter from him. He had refused to declare bankruptcy. He went back into business and paid off every cent he owed.

"I look back at the years before I underwent a character change," he wrote to me, "and I realize that I was really an obnoxious person. My wife must really have loved me to stay with me. I was insensitive and inconsiderate. I was opinionated. There was only one right way to do things and that was my way. I was intolerant of anyone and anything that did not fit in the narrow parameters of my ideas. Whatever tolerance I had was based on your constitutional right to be stupid.

"The change in me since I realized that I gotta get outta my way has been revolutionary. I used to be grumpy and constantly discontented. I have no doubt that this was the reason for my high blood pressure. Today I am much more relaxed. My high blood pressure medication has been cut back sharply.

"Before I retire at night, I go through a list. Do I owe anyone an apology? Have I kept something secret that I should have shared? Was I kind and considerate? Did I do something for others today? Then, when I recite the Shema, I forgive everyone who may have offended me in any way.

"I have asked my wife, 'How and why did you put up with me?' She said, 'I knew that there was a beautiful person inside of you, but the alcohol locked him up, and that when you would stop drinking, that beautiful personality would emerge, and I prayed for that day.'

"My wife was naive. True, no changes can occur as long as alcohol is in the picture, but just stopping the drinking does not make the change. It takes much work and overcoming enormous resistance to eliminate character defects that have been embedded for years. Even then, it's an ongoing job because the old traits try to emerge. One must be on the alert. For me, I found that regular attendance at the recovery meetings prevented my regressing into my old, obnoxious personality."

Alone or Lonely

One would think that with the unprecedented comforts and conveniences that modern science and technology have delivered, we would be riding on a crest of happiness.

Growing up in the 1930s, I knew a world in which life was difficult. Prior to the advent of antibiotics, the average life expectancy was fifty. Every major city had a tuberculosis sanitarium, and this disease cut people's lives short in their thirties. There was no immunization. Our house was quarantined when I had all the childhood diseases: measles, chicken pox, scarlet fever, mumps, whooping cough. A backache in the summer brought the dread of polio.

In absence of air-conditioning, we suffered in sweltering heat. There were no electronics to make work easy. The kitchen was a workplace: no fast or frozen foods, no microwave ovens, few takeouts. Laundry was done on a scrubbing board.

Travel was a chore. There were no jet planes, so New York to California took sixty hours by train. My first car was a 1936 Plymouth, no power steering, no power brakes, no air-conditioning. There was no television, no smartphones, no computers.

If people in the 1930s had been told what life would be like in the twenty-first century, they would not have believed it possible, but might have said, "If that materializes, we will have Paradise on earth."

What is the twenty-first century Paradise? The drug epidemic killing off youth, depression and anxiety rampant. Billions of doses of tranquilizers and antidepressants swallowed to escape the misery of "Paradise."

Rehabilitation centers flourish because addictions are on the increase. The number of children growing up in a single-parent home is unprecedented.

That is not the way the world was intended to be. Instead of a genuine happiness, we have a counterfeit happiness. Instead of a real "self," we have a pseudo-self, and we have been deluded into believing it's real.

Technology has improved communication...or has it? One can see a group of teenagers hanging out together, essentially ignoring each other's presence as they punch the keys to send text messages. The emotional bonds in face-to-face contact have been eliminated by electronics.

Aloneness is a state of absence of people. Sitting in a stadium among fifty thousand people, one is certainly not alone, but one can be terribly lonely. Aloneness is when you don't have other people, *loneliness is when you don't have yourself,* and a counterfeit self is as worthless as counterfeit money.

I have treated thousands of alcoholics and drug addicts and witnessed the miracle of recovery. For the first time, they become aware of their emotions, which had been numbed by chemicals. In recovery group meetings, they share their emotions amid both genuine laughter and tears.

If a person thought himself wealthy because he had millions of dollars, and then he discovers that these were worthless counterfeit bills, he is in the position of the addict who reaches "rock bottom." He must dispose of the bogus money, and only when he gets the counterfeit money "outta his way" can he begin to accumulate things of real value.

Rebbe Nachman of Breslov describes bouts of severe depression. "There were times when I felt I was in the depths of Hell, but even then I was not alone. The Psalmist says, 'If I ascend to Heaven, You are there; if I make my bed in the lowest depths, behold, You are there' (*Tehillim* 139:8). Even in the depths of Hell, I was not alone, because Hashem was with me. The pseudo-self repels the Divine presence. With the real self, one is neither alone nor lonely."

Lying – the Greatest Obstacle

I have told people who claim to be sincere in wishing to stop drinking, using drugs, or any other addiction, that there is an effective shortcut to overcoming the addiction: stop lying! It is virtually impossible to continue the addiction if one is absolutely truthful. The role of *emes* is so crucial that it deserves some elaboration.

Emes is that which attracts Hashem's presence, because the prophet says that *emes* is the Name of Hashem (*Yirmiyahu* 10:10).

The overriding importance of *emes* can be gathered from the fact that the Torah doesn't prescribe precautionary regulations to avoid committing sins. Those measures were formulated by the Sages. For example, the Scriptural prohibition is not to eat meat cooked with milk. The Sages prescribed precautionary measures, such as to keep meat and dairy strictly separated, and they extended the ban to poultry as well. Scripture forbids certain types of work on Shabbos, and the Sages added the precautionary measure of *muktzeh*.

Only in one place does Scripture itself prescribe a precautionary law. Not only does the Torah forbid lying (*Vayikra* 19:11), it goes beyond that to say, "*Distance yourself from falsehood"* (*Shemos* 23:7), i.e., do not do anything that may lead to a lie. If one does something that one may have to deny having done, one has already violated a Scriptural prohibition.

If there is anything our tzaddikim did to the extreme, it was their unshakable adherence to *emes*. Some even refused to use the word *emes* in ordinary conversation because it is the name of Hashem. Rather, they would use the Yiddish-German word for truth, *wahrheit*. Many times I heard them say *"es is wuhr"* for "it is true." They said that the verse we translate as, "Distance yourself from falsehood," can also be translated as, "With falsehood you distance yourself from Hashem."

When the Chafetz Chaim published the first volume of his epochal *Mishnah Berurah*, he traveled to various towns to distribute it. He would also lecture in these towns. In one town, he noticed the announcement of his speech as being given by "the author of *Mishnah Berurah*." He took his pen and added "of the first volume" lest people come to the erroneous conclusion that he had completed the entire work.

The father of the *maggid* Rav Yitzchak of Drohovitz was known as "Reb Yosef the truthful one" because he never deviated from the truth. One day a local merchant asked a favor of him. "I have some contraband merchandise, and if the government inspectors find it, I can be exiled to Siberia for life. I would like to leave it with you. If you tell them that you have no contraband, they will believe you."

Reb Yosef asked the merchant how much the contraband was worth. He said, "Fifty rubles," which was an appreciable sum. Reb Yosef borrowed fifty rubles, bought the contraband, and set fire to it. He was not going to lie to the inspectors (*Mi'Dvar Sheker Tirchak*, p.106).

A chassid of Rebbe Refael of Bershad gave the Rebbetzin a gift of a silver-plated menorah. When Rebbe Refael saw it on Friday night, he said to the Rebbetzin, "Why do we have to indulge in luxury?"

The Rebbetzin said, "It is not real silver, only silver-plated."

Rebbe Refael said, "Then it is both excessive luxury and deceptive," and disposed of it.

Emes was of such great importance to Rebbe Refael that when he heard that a child of his had told a lie, he sat shivah for him, mourning him as though he had died.

There was a case in which a Jew was accused of cheating the government and was in danger of lifelong imprisonment. The court said that if two prominent rabbis would testify to the man's honesty, the charges would be dropped. One of the two rabbis was Rebbe Refael.

Rebbe Refael was in a dilemma. To refuse to testify for the man was tantamount to saying that he is dishonest. However, to testify that he is an honest person would be a lie. The night before the trial, Rebbe Refael prayed tearfully to Hashem to deliver him from this dilemma, and he died amid his tearful prayers.

Rav Yechezkel Levenstein was a close friend of Rav Yitzchak Eizik Schor. When the latter died, it was assumed that Rav Yechezkel would eulogize him. To everyone's surprise, Rav Yechezkel refused to do so. He later explained that shortly prior to that, he had lost a dear grandchild. "I was concerned that in the eulogy I might think about my grandchild for whom I am in grief, and I might cry. The audience would assume that I was grieving over Rav Yitzchak Eizik, and that would be dishonest of me."

When Rav Eliyahu Lopian would serve as *shaliach tzibbur*

on the *yamim tovim* and come to the words, "Behold, I am impoverished of good deeds, and I stand frightened and trembling before Hashem," he would omit the words "I stand frightened and trembling before Hashem" — "How can I say that when it is not true?"

We find something similar in the Talmud. Moshe said that Hashem is "great, mighty, and awesome" (*Devarim* 10:17). The *navi* Yirmiyahu refused to say "mighty" — "Where is His might? Heathens are dancing in His sanctuary." Daniel refused to say "awesome" — "Nations are oppressing His children. Where is His awesomeness?" The Talmud says that Yirmiyahu and Daniel knew that Hashem was mighty and awesome, but because they knew that Hashem was Absolute Truth, and they could not see His might and awesomeness, they did not believe it was right to say it (*Yoma* 69b). If one is dedicated to truth, intellectual knowledge is not enough. One must have an intense emotional sensation, equivalent to seeing it with one's eyes.

Because Rav Lopian knew how dear truth is to Hashem, he did not want to say words that he felt were not true of him.

I must interject here a personal achievement of which I am both proud and ashamed. I am proud that I have avoided lying, but I am ashamed of how this came about. The Torah says, "You shall not lie" (*Vayikra* 19:11), yet, like many people, I skirted the truth a bit. For example, when you do not attend a friend's wedding because you were not in the mood, and your friend later asks you why you were not at the wedding, you don't admit that you just did not feel like it. Rather, you make up some excuse like, "I'm terribly sorry, but I had to take my mother-in-law to the doctor's office," which is a lie. We frequently rationalize telling "white lies," although there is nothing in halachah that justifies this.

I was privileged to receive a very important personal teaching that has profoundly affected my lifestyle as well as my therapeutic technique.

I had a patient who was a chronic complainer, coming up with new physical symptoms frequently. I felt that his complaints were nothing but malingering, an effort to get additional medication. I wrote an order for the nurse to give him a placebo injection of 1 cc. of saltwater. The nurse told me that she could not follow that order because, by the order of the clinical director, we were not allowed to use placebo medications. This was strange, because when I was an intern in general medicine we had used placebos when we thought the patient was feigning pain.

I asked the clinical director, who was my mentor, for the reason prohibiting the use of placebos. Although he ascribed to the theory of evolution, his reasoning still has merit. He said, "Abe, long before man developed the ability to speak, we communicated the way animals do, by scents, body language, and a variety of other nonverbal methods.

"When we developed verbal communication, that was superimposed upon the older, nonverbal forms, but it did not eliminate them. Even now, we communicate nonverbally. It is just that our conscious verbal communication obscures the nonverbal communication of the subconscious mind.

"You have conscious control of what you say, but you do not have voluntary control over your nonverbal communication. If you give the patient a placebo, your verbal communication is, 'I am giving you something,' but your nonverbal communication is, 'I am giving you nothing.' You are sending your patient contradictory messages, which diminishes his trust in you and undermines the doctor-patient relationship, which is the only tool we have in psychotherapy."

The fact that there was Creation rather than evolution does not alter things. I believed my mentor was right and concluded that I couldn't lie, not only because it is ethically wrong, but because I can't be a good liar. If I lie to someone, my conscious mind will lie, and the listener's conscious mind will hear it, but both of our subconscious minds will communicate and receive the truth, and my involuntary nonverbal communication will betray the truth. Ever since then, I have avoided "white lies." These are easy to justify, but they can subvert any meaningful relationship.

Perhaps the words of the Torah, *"lo teshakru,"* should not be translated as "You *shall* not lie," but rather, "You *cannot* lie."

Some people think they can get away with lying. It may work for the short term, but the long-term effects are detrimental to any relationship.

Complacency

Working with people in recovery has broadened my perspective. Alcoholism is a destructive lifestyle that can serve as a model for other lifestyles destructive in their own way. Just as the alcoholic is in denial and cannot see the harm of his lifestyle, so it is with many people who are not addicts. They are complacent, satisfied with their status quo, just like the cigarette smoker who does not realize that the tiny lung cancer is ebbing away his life. It takes a "rock-bottom" experience to shake a person out of his complacency.

A striking example of how a rock-bottom experience can change a person's lifestyle is the following testimony of a recovering alcoholic, a forty-six-year-old successful board-certified neurosurgeon.

"My moment of truth occurred in a small-town prison cell, where I woke up after a bout of heavy drinking. My head was pounding as if an air hammer was hitting it, and my stomach was afire. 'Where am I?' I called out. 'Is anyone here?' but no one responded. I was left alone in my pain and utter confusion. It was an unforgettable experience, and I pray that I should never forget it.

"After what seemed like a century of torture, the jailer showed up. 'Where am I?' I asked, 'and how did I get here?'

"The jailer told me the name of a small village, about fifty miles from my home. 'A state trooper found you passed out in your car. Your car went off the road. You're lucky to be alive.' Then the jailer said, 'Your ID says you're a doctor. You don't look like a doctor to me. You look like a common drunk.'

"No words in the English language could have penetrated like these. Everything I had worked for in my life, everything I had aspired to since my childhood came crashing down like a house of cards.

"My father was a well-liked family physician, but I was going to outdo him. I was going to be a respected surgeon, driving a luxury car, the envy of everyone. I was going to make my impact on society. But it all faded away. I was a common drunk, and my luxury sedan was abandoned off a country road. No doubt the local paper would flash the headline, 'Prominent Neurosurgeon Jailed for Drunk Driving.' I had expended all my efforts to be a somebody and ended up worse than a nobody.

"I was mandated to a rehab facility, following which I had to attend AA and be monitored. I was on probation at the hospital. For some reason, people were uncomfortable with a drunk poking around inside their brain.

"The rehab opened my eyes to the phoniness of my search for power and prestige, but the true realization took place in the AA meetings. I was respected as just "Ed," a recovering alcoholic. My status as a neurosurgeon did not count. I got a cup of coffee no different than a guy on welfare. I could not boast about my Lexus, because my driver's license was lifted (I had two previous DUIs). I was just another drunk who wanted to regain control of my life. I wanted to live my life for myself rather than for what other people would think of me. Today is four years since I reached the moment of truth in the jail cell. I am back in my practice, and I am grateful that people have the trust to allow this ex-common drunk to poke around in their brain. I feel more comfortable with my identity as an ex-common drunk than as a prestigious doctor."

It took an ego-shattering experience to bring this man out of a lethal complacency.

Did He Really Have a Way?

I understand what the recovered alcoholic meant by, "I've gotta get outta my way," but I want to focus on a technicality. Did he really have a way?

I raise this issue because of an explanation by one of the commentaries on a verse in *Tehillim*. The Psalmist compares the lifestyle of a Torah-observant person to that of a sinful person and concludes, "For Hashem attends *the way* of the righteous, while *the way* of the *rasha* will perish" (*Tehillim* 1:6). The commentary asks, "Can it be said of a *rasha* that he has a way at all?"

I can appreciate this comment because I lived in Pittsburgh, famous for having "a bridge to nowhere." There are several "bridges to nowhere" in different parts of the world. I don't recall the history of the Pittsburgh bridge. There was an article in a Pittsburgh newspaper, which wrote that the term "bridge to nowhere" is an oxymoron. A bridge, by definition, is a structure that provides a span from one place to another. If it does not do so, it cannot be referred to as a bridge, only as a structure that was intended to become a bridge but never made it.

This is also true of a "way." If one tosses up a bunch of

coins that fall to the ground, one cannot say that each coin had a "way" where to fall. Hundreds of ants in an anthill may seem to be moving at random, but they do have a "way," even if they are guided by instinct. The coins are not directed at all.

I sat with my father in the hospital when he was receiving chemotherapy for pancreatic cancer. He looked out the window at the busy traffic, with cars weaving in and out, trying to get a few feet ahead, risking their lives for the questionable gain of a few seconds. He was at the stage of seriously considering what life is all about, and remarked, "What a foolish world."

Charles Schulz has a charming cartoon wherein Sally says to Charlie Brown, "Wake up, big brother."

Charlie sits up, saying, "Wake up? What for?"

Sally says, "So you can get an early start."

Charlie says, "I'm not going anywhere."

Sally says, "That's a shame. You could have been the first one there."

This is the mentality that merited my father's observation, "What a foolish world." You need not have a goal at all, but just being first has value, even if there's nothing to be first at.

That is our modern culture: speed has a value, even if one achieves nothing. "Reasonable" people can be convinced to spend many more thousands of dollars for an automobile that can go "from zero to sixty miles per hour in 4.7 seconds." The fact that there is no place where one can put this marvelous triumph of technology to use is no deterrent.

The alcoholic may give the impression of having a "way" and may be working at a frenetic pace. He may even amass a great deal of money, but it is all an illusion. I have treated alcoholics and drug addicts who were immensely wealthy, but they were miserable. Their wealth and social status gave them a spurious identity.

Among my favorite folktales are the stories of the "Wise Men of Chelm." These stories are about a group of villagers who were remarkably simple in a quaint sort of way.

Psychology stresses the importance of having an identity. Psychotherapists often try to help people "find themselves." A popular psychological theme is "Who am I really?" This story of the Wise Men of Chelm lends a perspective to this issue.

> *One day, a citizen of Chelm was at the public bathhouse. It suddenly dawned upon him that without clothes, most people look alike. He became quite anxious at the thought of, "When it comes time to go home, how will I know which one is me?"*
>
> *After pondering this a bit, he came up with a brilliant solution. He found a piece of red string and tied it around his big toe. He was now distinctly identifiable.*
>
> *Unfortunately, in the process of sudsing and showering, the red string fell off his foot, and when another bather stepped on it, it stuck to his foot.*
>
> *When it was time to leave, the first bather looked at his foot, and seeing nothing on it, was perplexed. Then he noticed the other man with the string on his foot. He approached him and said, "I know who you are, but can you tell me, who am I?"*

Some people seek an identity by having the equivalent of a red string. Their identity is the luxury automobile in the driveway or the impressive facade on their mansion. But this is hardly an internal identity. What happens if one sells the car? Does the identity go along with it?

It's not much different if one's identity is, "I am a doctor" or, "I am a lawyer." That is a description of what one *does* rather than what one *is*. If one's only identity is, "I am a doctor," then one shares an identity with myriads of other doctors, but one does not have an individual identity of one's own.

Abstinence Is Not Sobriety

An alcoholic may stop drinking because his doctor told him that his liver is seriously damaged, and any further drinking will kill him. If he does nothing more than abstain from alcohol, he is what is considered "a dry drunk." Alcoholics generally have many character defects, and these remain when he stops drinking. The wife of one "dry drunk" said, "I wish he'd start drinking again. He was easier to live with."

One alcoholic, on his thirty-fifth anniversary of sobriety said, "The man I once was, drank, and the man I once was will drink again. If I ever go back to being the selfish, inconsiderate person I once was, I will drink again."

This applies to all faulty behavior. Rambam says that Hashem forgives when a person does the kind of *teshuvah* that enables him to say, "I am no longer the person that committed the sin. I am a different person."

Character defects are deeply ingrained in one's personality and are not easily eliminated. Rav Yisrael of Salant said, "It is easier to complete the entire Talmud than to correct even a single character defect."

Rav Chaim Vital, successor to the Ari, said that a person

should exercise greater care about a character defect than with Scriptural prohibitions, because a sin, even a grievous sin, does not become part of a person's personality, whereas a character defect, such as going into rage, becomes part of a person's nature and is much more difficult to correct. Yet it's not uncommon for a person who is meticulous about his standards of kashrus to retain resentment toward someone who offended him.

I have seen alcoholics disclose their character defects and ask for help with them. The 12-step program requires that a person do as much as is humanly possible to correct a character defect. Only when one has done so can one pray for God to eliminate the character defect. This is what the recovering addict meant when he said, "My recovery is a miracle. There is no way I could have done this. I know that God did this. I just had to get out of His way."

Wholeness

The *sifrei mussar* speak about the importance of *shleimus*. Optimum functioning can be obtained only when there is *shleimus*. A person with a physical defect may be performing at a very high level, perhaps even higher than people without a defect, as is evident from people who made great accomplishments in spite of significant limitations. In fact, some people have achieved excellence *because* of their physical defects, when they compensated for their defect by pushing their other abilities to the fullest. Nevertheless, for the average person, a significant defect may compromise one's ability to achieve the highest degree of excellence. Yet a person with a physical defect, even a significant defect, is not in any way a lesser human being. The physical defect does not detract from one's menschhood.

On the other hand, a person who lacks the essential features of the spirit, the unique traits that distinguish man from other living things, is lacking in menschhood. This is why the Talmud says that *resha'im* are considered dead even though they are physically alive (*Berachos* 18b). *Resha'im* live only to satisfy their physical desires. Their animal component is very much alive, but their human component, the spirit, is dead. Hence, a person who is physically impaired is still a whole mensch, whereas if one has significant defects of the spirit, one cannot be whole.

It is more than a play on words that *shaleim* (whole) and *shalom* (peace) are almost identical. One can be happy and at peace with oneself only when one is *shaleim*. Paradoxically, some people think they are in pursuit of happiness, when, in fact, they are in pursuit of misery. The classic example of this is the drug addict, who "pursues happiness" with drugs, which causes him only misery and even death.

Rebbe Levi Yitzchak of Berditchev stopped a man who was hurrying through the marketplace. "I'm sorry, Rebbe," the man said. "I can't talk with you now. I'm after my *parnasah*." Rebbe Levi Yitzchak said, "How do you know that your *parnasah* is in the direction in which you are running? Maybe your *parnasah* is in the opposite direction, and you are running away from it."

A recovered cocaine addict said, "The worst day of my sobriety is better than the best day of my addiction," but this is not what he thought when he was using cocaine. Addicts are not the only people mistaken in thinking that they are in pursuit of happiness. People who sacrifice their spirit to satisfy their body are making the same mistake.

One of the unique human traits that distinguishes man from other living things is that a person has the capacity to voluntarily improve himself. *Kol hakavod* to those who exercise regularly to improve their body strength, but we must similarly improve the spirit component.

Rav Saadia Gaon once lodged at an inn, and the innkeeper did not recognize his famous guest. When someone who did recognize him told the innkeeper whom he had the great privilege to host, the innkeeper apologized profusely to the *gaon*. Rav Saadia said, "There is no reason to apologize. You treated me with great respect." The innkeeper said, "But if I had known who you were, I would have treated you as befits your lofty position."

Rav Saadia broke into tears. "I thought my worship of Hashem yesterday was appropriate. But my awareness of the infinite greatness of Hashem is more today. Had I known yesterday what I know today, the quality of my worship would have been much better."

Developing spirituality is an uphill drive, and if one does not move upward, one will slide back down. If one has not advanced spiritually, then one has actually regressed.

We stop growing physically in early adulthood. Neurologists say our mental acuity begins to decrease when we consider ourselves at the prime of life. But even loss of some brain cells should not impede one's spiritual growth.

The Talmud relates that the great sage, Rabi Eliezer, fell seriously ill, and his students came to comfort him. One student said, "Our master! You are dearer to us than a father and mother. A father and mother can provide a child only with This World, but you, our master, have provided us with the World to Come." Rabi Eliezer did not acknowledge this student's comment.

Another student said, "Our master! You are dearer to us than the sun. The sun can provide a person only with This World, but you, our master, have provided us with the World to Come." Rabi Eliezer remained silent.

A third student said, "Our master! You are dearer to us than the rain. The rain can provide a person only with This World, but you, our master, have provided us with the World to Come." Again, Rabi Eliezer remained silent.

Then Rabi Akiva spoke up. "Suffering can be precious," he said.

Rabi Eliezer said, "Help me sit up so that I can better hear what my child, Akiva, has to say."

All the other students had said things that should have comforted Rabi Eliezer. Why did he ignore them and listen only to Rabi Akiva?

Resting on one's laurels is vanity and achieves nothing. Rabi Eliezer valued life because it provided him with the opportunity to do Hashem's Will. But he was now weak and bedridden and could do nothing. This depressed him, and the fact that he had achieved much in the past did not comfort him in the least. He could be comforted only if there were something he could do now.

What Rabi Akiva said was that the Divine Will is that a person should maximize oneself spiritually. This is what man was created for, and maximizing oneself is self-fulfillment, which is the only thing Rabi Eliezer felt was of value. However, in his condition, he did not see what he could do that would be spiritually fulfilling.

Rabi Akiva said that self-fulfillment consists of doing whatever one can do *at any particular moment, given one's condition at that moment*. Essentially, what he told the master was, "When you had the ability to teach, your self-fulfillment was teaching. Your condition now does not permit you to do that or anything else that you consider important. All you can do now is accept your suffering with trust and faith in Hashem, and when you do that, you are fulfilling yourself every bit as much as when you taught us."

This was a role reversal, with the student teaching his teacher. The point is significant. We can fulfill ourselves at any stage in life and under all circumstances. Rabi Eliezer was whole when he was healthy and robust and also when he was weak and bedridden.

Nothing need stand in the way of improving the traits

that comprise the spirit. Being compassionate and considerate is a spiritual trait, and one can always increase one's compassion. As one exercises and improves a spiritual trait, one's *shleimus* and wholeness become more complete.

Choosing What's Right

A crucial distinction between man and animals is the ability to choose. Animals have no choice because they are dominated by their physical drives. A human being is a *bocher* (a chooser) and can resist yielding to a drive if he thinks it's wrong or harmful.

Yetzias Mitzrayim is a pillar of Yiddishkeit, because that is when we emerged as a nation, capable of receiving the Torah. Yet one may wonder why we so often mention Yetzias Mitzrayim. No nation celebrates their independence for a whole week, with the many restrictions that Pesach has. Furthermore, we commemorate Yetzias Mitzrayim every Friday night and every festival at Kiddush. Tefillin is a daily reminder of Yetzias Mitzrayim, and many mitzvos refer to Yetzias Mitzrayim. Even given its historic importance, this seems like overkill.

I gained an understanding into this from a man who was a severe drug addict for many years. He told me that at the first Seder he attended when sober, he interrupted his father when the latter began reciting "*Avadim Hayinu.*"

He said, "Abba, can you truthfully say that you were a slave? Yes, our ancestors were slaves, but you have no idea what it feels like to be a slave. *I* can tell you what it feels like to be a slave. For twenty-two years I was a slave to drugs. I did things I never thought I could do, but I had no choice. Drugs were my taskmasters, and I had to do what the drugs demanded. Today, I am a *ben chorin*, a free person."

This man gave me a precious insight. Yetzias Mitzrayim is much more than a national event. A person can be a slave to a despot like Pharaoh, but one can also be a slave to the deadly habit of cigarettes or the addiction to alcohol or other chemicals. One can be a slave to compulsive gambling or to lustful behavior. A person who has no control of his anger is a slave to it, as is a person who is a slave to *kavod*. A person with a compulsive eating disorder is a slave. Indeed, a person who goes on vacation and must contact his office multiple times a day is a slave to his office.

We frequently mention Yetzias Mitzrayim to remind us of the pivotal importance of being a *ben chorin*. If we lose our freedom to make choices because of compulsions, we have lost a vital component of our humanity.

You may say, "Yes, but upon Yetzias Mitzrayim Hashem said, '*avadai heim* — they are My slaves.' Isn't accepting the yoke of Torah a form of slavery?" The answer is yes, but I am free to choose this subjugation every day when I say *Shema Yisrael*. We couldn't choose whether to accept the yoke of Pharaoh, and when one is an addict to anything, one has no choice to resist the compulsion.

Bechirah is the hallmark of humanity, and it's so sad to see intelligent people fall into the trap of slavery and lose their uniqueness as human beings.

Personal desires are an obstacle to *bechirah*. The Torah says that a judge who accepts a bribe is "blinded" by it and cannot possibly be objective. Inasmuch as we are all subject to personal desires, what can we do to avoid making wrong choices?

This question was posed to Rebbe Yisrael of Ruzhin. He suggested, "Observe a tightrope walker, who must maintain a sensitive balance to avoid falling to his death. If he feels a tug to the right, he leans a bit to the left, and vice versa. Similarly, when you have a strong desire to do something, pause and think of reasons why you should *not* do it. That may enable you to be more objective."

Chesed

We achieve wholeness by being everything that we can be. In high school, a buddy of mine and I took a test on which he received an A- and I received a C+. We compared the two tests, and they were essentially equivalent. I asked the instructor why I got a lower grade. He answered, "Because I expected more from you."

If we do not live up to our potential, we are remiss and lacking in wholeness.

We all do much *tzedakah and chesed*, but if we wish to improve ourselves spiritually, we should see whether we are indeed living up to our ability to do *chesed*. Our tzaddikim can serve as models for us. While we may not be able to reach their lofty levels, they can inspire us to greater achievement.

A ten-year-old boy was doing well in his violin lessons. When violin virtuoso Itzhak Perlman came to town, the boy's father took his son to the concert. The child was enchanted by the artist's performance. On the way out, the father asked the child, "Do you think you will ever be able to perform like Itzhak Perlman?"

The child said, "Maybe not, but I'm going to practice more."

To Rebbe Meir Horowitz of Tiktin, *chesed* was not just a mitzvah, it was his oxygen. He would not eat anything unless he had had a chance to do *chesed* that day. One day, no opportunity to do *chesed* presented itself, and by late afternoon he had not yet eaten, so he went into the marketplace to find an opportunity to do *chesed*.

It was late in the day, and most merchants had packed up their merchandise. One lumber merchant had a load of wood and said he was willing to sell it at a low price. Rebbe Meir ran to the local carpenter. "I think I have a *metziah* for you," he said, and escorted him to the marketplace. The carpenter confirmed that this was indeed a *metziah*, but unfortunately he didn't have the money to take advantage of it. "Wait here," Rebbe Meir said. He ran home and then returned, bringing money that he lent the carpenter, who bought the lumber. Having done *chesed*, Rebbe Meir then went home to eat.

Rebbe Ze'ev of Zebarazh was hosting several friends at a meal. It was a cold winter day, and it occurred to him that the coach driver was out in the cold. He quickly *bentshed* and went out to the driver. "Go inside and warm up," he said. "I'll watch the horses." When Rebbe Ze'ev did not return for a long time, his friends went out and found Rebbe Ze'ev shivering in the cold, as the driver had fallen asleep in the warm house.

One of the reasons the 12-step program is effective in eliminating character defects is because it mandates that a recovering addict should help active addicts recover. This is an act of *chesed*, and it's referred to as doing "12th-step work."

An alcoholic was admitted to the detox unit at four a.m. He told me that, in desperation, he had called the AA hotline late at night, and that at midnight an AA person, Darin, came to his home and sat with him for two hours trying to convince him to go to the hospital. At four a.m. Darin helped him pack, drove him to the hospital, and stayed with him until he was admitted.

I was able to identify Darin. He is a high-priced attorney. A consultation in his office during the day would have cost three hundred dollars an hour. But Darin went to this man's house at midnight, spent several hours with him, and drove him to the hospital. I'm sure that Darin later called the AA office to thank them for giving him the opportunity to help someone. That is the magic of *chesed*.

Practicing *chesed* is meritorious in its own right. It counteracts the character defects of selfishness and inconsiderateness. But it also can eliminate other character defects.

A woman noticed that a chair in her living room was very shabby, and she bought a new chair. But then this caused the sofa, by contrast, to look very unattractive. When she replaced the sofa, the carpet appeared ugly, and the new carpet clashed with the old drapes. In short, the entire living room went through an overhaul because one piece of furniture was replaced.

This is also true of character defects. Correcting one defect may bring to the fore the unacceptability of other character traits that had heretofore gone unnoticed. In due time, a beautiful personality replaces the negative traits. This is true of all faulty personalities, not only that of the addict.

Perspective

Perspective is a tricky issue. The idea of "living one day at a time" antedated the 12-step program by centuries. The Psalmist says, "Even today, if we but heed His call" (*Tehillim* 98:7). *Kerem Shlomo* comments that the strategy of the *yetzer hara* is to tell you, "There is no way you can observe all these mitzvos and prohibitions for the rest of your life. Why fight a losing battle?" The rebuttal to the *yetzer hara* is, "I don't have to be concerned about the rest of my life. I just need to observe the mitzvos today, and that is easily doable. I'll deal with tomorrow's challenges tomorrow."

On the other hand, the *yetzer hara* will tempt you to satisfy your momentary pleasure now and pay no attention to the future consequences. We must conceptualize the world as a temporary experience, and we must live in a way so as to assure our eternal life in Gan Eden. Animals have no perspective and do whatever will satisfy their bodily drive at the moment.

Again, addiction can serve as a model. The addict is motivated by instantaneous pleasure. That is why addicts are not discouraged by the fact that drugs will destroy their future. The addict has no concept of future. The "future" he is concerned about is measurable in seconds or in minutes at the most. How drugs may ruin his future is of no concern to him, because "future" is an alien concept.

Many people who are not addicts may also have no perspective. All their lives are based on the "here and now." They make major decisions without giving much, if any, consideration to how their decision will affect their future.

Staying Outta My Way

Whereas getting outta my way was a challenge, I was helped to do so by a powerful teacher: *"rock bottom."*

Self-deception can go only so far. Rock bottom is a hard teacher, but addicts will learn no other way. We had to give up our will, because we saw where that got us. Loss after loss after loss. Rock bottom is an individual phenomenon. One person's rock bottom may not be anything for another person.

Jim C. was a bright young man, and he took a position in a major construction firm. He denied he was an alcoholic because he only drank beer. When Jim's wife told him that she could not tolerate his drinking, he told her that she was free to leave. She indeed did so, taking their three daughters and moving in with her parents.

Jim was exceptionally resourceful and received promotion after promotion, becoming the assistant to the CEO at an unprecedented young age. Eventually, his drinking resulted in work impairment, but Jim disregarded all warnings, saying, "You're just jealous of my success," until one day the CEO fired him.

He had lost his family and now his job. He drank away his savings, then drank away his house and car. At age forty-nine he admitted himself for detoxification, but left the hospital the very next day. Two years later, at age fifty-one, Jim readmitted himself for detox. "I'll do anything you tell me," Jim said.

I asked Jim, "Why are you more ready now than two years ago?"

Jim said, "Do you know what you get for selling your blood? Sixteen beers."

I said, "Selling your blood for beer is your rock bottom, huh?"

Jim said, "I guess not. I've been doing it for a year."

I said, "Then why are you here today?"

Jim said, "When I was with the firm, I ran the United Way drive single-handedly for two years. This week, I panhandled quarters on Liberty Avenue. I can't live like that."

Jim suffered many severe losses, but none of these were his rock bottom. Panhandling was more than he could take.

Jim recovered and was sober for twelve years, serving as a housekeeper for a church. Jim's rock bottom was severe enough that he did not relapse.

But some alcoholics relapse even after a severe rock bottom. They "get in their way" again.

The most common cause for relapse is the delusion that they can control alcohol again. Having suffered severe losses and having been sober for several years, they think they won't drink excessively again and that they no longer need the support of the AA fellowship. Their ego gets in their way. Staying outta one's way and avoiding relapse may, therefore, be more difficult than getting outta one's way initially, because there may not be the rock-bottom phenomenon that led to the initial recovery.

No Torah-Secular Dichotomy

Some people make the serious mistake of restricting religion to ritual, but do not subject daily behavior to Torah. They observe the laws of kashrus because that is religion, but they think that commercial transactions and other non-ritual acts do not fall under the rubric of religion. The Talmud says that there is one verse upon which *all* of Torah observance depends: "Know Hashem in all your ways" (*Mishlei* 3:6; *Berachos* 63). If one does not transact according to halachah, one is as much in violation of Torah as if one consumed *treif* food. Wholeness cannot be fragmented.

A number of years ago, I wrote the book *The Shame Borne in Silence*[1] in which I discussed the occurrence of domestic violence among Jews, and that this can occur even in Torah-observant families. Halachah dictates that spouses should relate to each other with utmost respect. People who abuse their spouses are no more Torah-observant than those who transgress other Torah prohibitions. (I was severely criticized, and some Judaica stores were forbidden by their rabbis to carry the book.)

---

[1] Abraham J. Twerski, *The Shame Borne in Silence* (Pittsburgh: Mirkov Publications, 1996).

Rage has nothing to do with ritual, and it's a grievous sin. The Talmud equates rage with the cardinal sins of idolatry, adultery, and murder. Rav Chaim Vital says that this is not just a figure of speech, but an actual assessment of the severity of rage.

When an epidemic of cholera broke out in Vilna, Rav Yisrael of Salant told the healthy students to care for the sick ones and to do whatever is necessary on Shabbos, looking away from the Shabbos prohibitions. One man expressed his appreciation to Rav Yisrael for the care given to his son, but added, "I think the students took too many liberties in doing forbidden things on Shabbos."

In something very uncharacteristic of Rav Yisrael, he shouted at the man at the top of his lungs, "Who are you to teach me halachah? These students were entrusted to me by their parents, and I am responsible for their health." Rav Yisrael later explained that because some students had overheard what this man had said and might refrain from doing things on Shabbos for the sick, he had to be unequivocal in ordering them not to be *"frum"* at the patients' expense. Nevertheless, this expression of anger haunted him for the rest of his life.

Rabbi Yitzchak Zilberstein cites a statement by Rav Chaim Vital about a person who did much *chesed* and anticipated that when he died, the gates of Heaven would swing wide open and he would be escorted directly to Avraham Avinu. Instead, he found the gates of Heaven tightly shut. He protested to the Heavenly Tribunal, "Where is the reward for all my *chesed*?"

The Tribunal answered, "We noted that you did no *chesed* at home. You were abusive and disrespectful toward your wife. If you did not behave with *chesed* toward your wife, all the *chesed* you did for others is of no account."

While the Chafetz Chaim greatly emphasized the importance of realizing the *kedushah* of Shabbos and the Talmudic statement that a public violation of Shabbos renders a person equal to an idol worshipper, and if he touches wine it becomes *treif* as if it had been handled by a non-Jew, nevertheless he threw all of his efforts into the elimination of *lashon hara*. Why? Because it is customary for a person to consult a *rav* about the permissibility of opening a can of sardines on Shabbos, but rarely does one ask a *rav* whether repeating something one heard about someone is permissible. People have great respect for Shabbos, but not for *lashon hara*.

Rashi points out that there are mitzvos that people treat lightly, as if they tread on them because they consider them insignificant. It is precisely careful observance of these mitzvos that warrants the *berachos* of Hashem (*Devarim* 7:12-16).

Sometimes a person fails to grasp the importance of a particular mitzvah. David HaMelech says, "The laws of Hashem are true, they are just taken all together" (*Tehillim* 19:10). If one isolates a particular mitzvah, one may not appreciate its meaning.

It Was Easier Back When

Having been in the psychiatric field for close to sixty years, I have had the opportunity of observing some changes in the way people think and behave.

The Torah relates that when Noach emerged from the ark, he planted a vineyard, made wine, got drunk, and behaved indecently. The obvious question is: How does a person whom the Torah considers a perfect tzaddik allow himself to get drunk?

The Sfas Emes provides the answer. Prior to the flood, Noach knew the amount of wine that he could consume safely. After the flood, he went back to drinking the same amount. What he did not realize was that it was not the same world. The flood had wiped out the earth's population. This was a new, different world, and the rules that prevailed in the previous world were no longer valid. When the world undergoes a radical change, one may have to adapt with new rules.

In 1972, I opened the Gateway Rehabilitation Center in Pittsburgh to treat chronic alcoholics. The average age of a patient was forty-five. This was likely a person who had suffered some consequences of his drinking: family breakup, physical disease, job loss, drunk-driving violations, etc. The addiction had beaten him up, and he was ready to surrender. There were a few drug addicts admitted, but they were in the minority.

The makeup of today's population is much different. We had to build a special wing to treat youngsters and provide knowledge and support for their families. In contrast to the forty-five-year-old alcoholic, these kids don't realize the horrible, self-destructive nature of their addiction. Even if they can be convinced of it, it is an intellectual awareness and does not have the impact of the consequences sustained by the forty-five-year-old alcoholic. The number of kids who die from drug overdose is unprecedented and frightening. The legalization of some drugs contributes to a permissive attitude.

Why are these young people not frightened off by the fear of death? Some continue use of drugs even after a close friend dies of an overdose. True, some youngsters think, *It won't happen to me. Jack just didn't know how to use the drug.* But the true reason is deeper than that.

When First Lady Nancy Reagan launched an anti-drug campaign with the slogan, "Just Say No," some people were interviewed about what they thought of this slogan. A fourteen-year-old girl said, "Why should I say no to drugs? What else is there?"

If youngsters feel that life offers them nothing worthwhile to live for, we can understand why the risk of dying does not frighten them.

This is a relatively new phenomenon. I am not a social scientist, so I cannot explain why so many young people are not sufficiently interested in life to avoid such high risk of death, especially with the lethal "designer drugs."

I have watched administration after administration wage war on drugs — harsh mandatory prison sentences, paying growers not to grow drugs, confiscating huge shipments of drugs, sniffing drugs at the airports, spending countless billions of dollars — all to no avail. The illegal drug business is thriving as never before, and this does not even take into account the massive amount of prescription drugs. It is clear to me that we will never curtail the use of drugs *until we have a satisfactory answer to the fourteen-year-old girl's question.* 'Why? What else is there?' Youngsters must have something to strive for in life.

While the drug problem is the most dramatic example of a destructive lifestyle, there are many others that are causing much harm. Family life has suffered drastically. Seventy years ago, divorce among Torah-observant families was a rarity. Today, it is a frequent occurrence, often before the first anniversary. The couple has not even had a chance to find out if they are compatible and whether they like each other! Their behavior reflects the intolerance and impatience of the drug addict who is driven by the desire for instant gratification, and at the slightest frustration they head for divorce. This selfishness would be despicable in its own right, but when innocent children are victims of the parents' impatience and lack of consideration, it is an unforgivable sin.

I've gotta get out of my way! What on earth is "the way" that is being obstructed? This leads to the question of what is the goal in life that a person should be pursuing.

A healthy person, whose eyes, ears, arms, and legs are functioning properly, has little chance of achieving happiness and a goal in life unless his mind is functioning the way a human mind should function. But if the human mind functions with the ideation and emotion of a chipmunk, he can have neither goals nor real happiness.

Mental activity can be divided into two major groups: intellect and affect (emotion). Animals don't have to think about a goal in life. They operate completely by instinct. Whatever intelligence they have, they use to satisfy their instinctual drives. It is a sad reflection on humanity that most people are no different. Yes, we have far superior intelligence. We can invent computers, smartphones, robots, microwaves, air-conditioning, and sundry other technological miracles, all of which may make our lives more comfortable, but these do not provide a goal in life.

What is a respectable goal for a human being, one that makes him qualitatively different from other living things? It is *to participate in one's creation*!

All other living things enter the world in a state of completion. They need only to grow. Some creatures, like butterflies and frogs, come into the world unfinished (as caterpillars or tadpoles), but their completion into butterflies and frogs is automatic. They do nothing volitionally to make the transformation. In fact, they are powerless to stop it, so they are really created complete.

Human beings are qualitatively different. We come into the world as little animals, and without conscious effort on our part, we would continue our existence and die as animals. Yes, we would be intelligent animals, but animals nevertheless.

What is the feature that makes us unique? It is *our ability to defy an animalistic drive*. Let's take a simple example. Hunger is an animal trait. People as well as animals experience hunger. However, animals must do something to quash their hunger, and must pursue getting food. They have no choice. A hungry animal cannot decide to fast. A person who is hungry is capable of resisting the drive for food, whether to control one's weight or as a religious duty. As he matures, man develops the ability to resist biological drives. The end product is not only an intelligent animal, but a being that is qualitatively different, *who has the ability to control his behavior*. This ability is not innate, and controlling one's behavior in defiance of biological drives — such as hunger, greed, anger, and lust — is something a person develops. Hence, a human being participates in his own unique formation.

If a person fails to develop the uniqueness of humanity, i.e., the ability to be master over one's biological drives, he is seriously remiss in his development and cannot be truthfully happy. Yes, a hedonist who satisfies every drive and desire may appear to be happy, but inasmuch as one is seriously lacking in one's humanity, one is a well-satiated glutton.

The "way" a person should pursue is to become the ideal human being. Yielding to all one's desires is a formidable obstacle to true happiness. He is akin to the heroin addict who nods off in what he feels is nirvana, but no self-respecting person would choose this brain-intoxicated pleasure as a goal in life, nor would one choose the hedonistic paradise of gluttony.

No sensible person would choose death and evil. The problem is that our perception is so distorted (remember Shlomo HaMelech: "All of a person's ways are proper in his own eyes") that we perceive evil as good and death as life. I regularly lecture to people, especially young people, "Do not choose a way of certain death," and yet some go on to destroy themselves with drugs. We are so tightly bound up with the pursuit of pleasure that we are blinded to the facts of reality. What is true of the drug addict's misperception that drugs are good is equally true of our misperception of other things in life. Our emotions rule our behavior, and we frequently choose curse and evil under the misconception that they are blessing and good.

Preparing for the Future

As I mentioned above, science tells us that man is *homo sapiens*, "a baboon with intelligence." I have a problem with that, because man is much more than an intelligent animal. Man's intellect allows him to commit atrocities that animals would never do. But what is worse, while man's intellect enables him to invent miraculous apparatus, it does not provide him with a concept of the future.

You will say, "That's not so. We have an elaborate Social Security system that enables younger people to provide for their old age, and there is an entire industry based on retirement. We are very conscious of the future."

True, but that is a very myopic consciousness, and we have it only because we see elderly people who cannot provide for themselves. We place ourselves in their position, and this enables us to think of ourselves in a similar state.

Periodically, I lecture to young drug addicts, and I say to them, "Can you think of yourself, where you would like to be ten years from now?" The blank expressions on their faces tell me I might just as well have been speaking in a foreign language. They had no idea what I am talking about. Their idea of "future" is limited to minutes, if not seconds.

I say to them, "Suppose I tell you that I have received a shipment of a great new drug from South America. It gives an unbelievable high, better than cocaine, heroin, and speed put together."

They say, "It must cost a bunch."

I say, "That's the best part of it. Two dollars a hit."

"Wow!" they say. "Give me a hundred dollars' worth!"

I say, "Gladly, but I don't want to deceive you. The high is out of this world. You've never had anything like it, but there's one thing. There's a lag period of forty-eight hours before the effect. Today is Tuesday. You take the drug today and you won't feel anything until Thursday night, but then it will propel you to outer space."

"Nothing until Thursday?"

"That's right."

"I don't want that kind of junk." And the addicts walk away.

The addict's myopic concept of future allows them to destroy their lives. This is something we should take into consideration in our own lives.

The Talmud says that had the Torah not been given to us, there are some modes of proper conduct we could learn from observing other creatures (*Eruvin* 100b). These are things animals do by instinct, but we should do them by exercising our intellect. Many animals prepare for the future. Squirrels "know" there will be a winter, when food will not be available, so they hoard a number of nuts beyond their actual needs.

We are taught that our existence in this earthly world is but a period in which we can prepare for the Next World. In our rather brief sojourn in This World, we must prepare not for a winter of several months, and not for a century, but for an existence of eternity. Our myopic vision gets in our way.

One Sukkos, I was asked, "If Sukkos is the festival of gladness, why did the Sages propose that we read Koheles, which is such a depressing book? Shlomo negates everything. Wealth, wisdom, fame, and glory all are 'hevel havalim,' absolute nothingness."

The answer is in the first chapter of *Mesillas Yesharim*. Ramchal points out that any thinking person could not possibly conclude that the reason for one's existence is just to enjoy earthly pleasures. There is far too much misery in the world, and if the purpose of Creation were physical pleasure, then Creation would be a terrible hoax.

Even in my own time, such a thought was inconceivable. I remember the discomforts of life before immunization, antibiotics, jet flight, air-conditioning, computers, Internet, microwaves, automatic washers and dryers, power steering and brakes, television, frozen foods, smartphones, etc. Before push-button electronics, work required physical exertion, and the average life expectancy in the US was below fifty. No one could think that the world was meant to be an amusement park, loaded with fun and pleasure.

Modern science and technology have eliminated many of the discomforts of daily life, and this has given rise to the idea that the purpose of life is getting maximum pleasure. When people, especially young people, do not have the pleasures they think is their due, they look for it in drugs.

In my fifty-plus years of psychiatric practice, I have witnessed the prevalence of depression due to the disappointment that people are not getting the expected pleasures of life. I see thousands of young men and women poisoning themselves with toxic chemicals to get pleasure or to be free of depression.

Satan has succeeded in deluding people that life was meant to be fun and pleasurable, and even bright people are taken in by this delusion.

There is a parable of a man who approached a group of

blind people and said loudly, "Here, I'm giving you a thousand dollars. Share it with your comrades," but he did not give anyone anything. The blind people, assuming that he gave one of them a thousand dollars to share, were bitterly disappointed when they did not receive anything. This is how Satan has deluded people to think they will receive the pleasures of life. I have seen many youngsters die from an overdose of drugs as a result of seeking the pleasures of life.

Several thousand years ago, Shlomo HaMelech put it to the test. Here is what he said:

I said to myself, Come, I will experiment with joy and enjoy pleasure. That, too, turned out to be futile.

I ventured to stimulate my body with wine — while my heart was involved with wisdom — and so to grasp folly, until I can discern which is best for mankind to do under the heavens during the brief span of their lives. I acted in grand style: I built myself houses; I planted vineyards; I made for myself gardens and orchards and planted in them every kind of fruit tree; I constructed pools from which to irrigate a grove of young trees; I bought slaves — male and female — and I acquired stewards; I also owned more possessions, both cattle and sheep, than all of my predecessors in Jerusalem; I amassed even silver and gold for myself and the treasure of kings and the provinces; I provided myself with various musical instruments and with every human luxury — chests and chests of them. Thus I grew and surpassed any of my predecessors in Jerusalem; still, my wisdom stayed with me. Whatever my eyes desired, I did not deny them; I did not deprive myself of any kind of joy. Indeed, my heart drew joy from all my activities, and this was my reward for all my endeavors.

Then I looked at all the things that I had done and the energy I had expended in doing them; it was clear that it was all futile and a vexation of the spirit — and there is no profit under the sun (Koheles 2:1-11).

Shlomo HaMelech was able to maintain his wisdom throughout the experiment. Today, people's pursuit of pleasure distorts their wisdom. The realization of the truth will come when we can no longer do anything about it.

Chronic Discontent

More than fifty-five years ago, I began my career in psychiatry. This was before the availability of antidepressants. We ascribed to whatever psychological theory seemed to be most sensible.

You might be interested in knowing how antidepressants came about. Like most other discoveries in medicine, antidepressants were not the result of a well-thought-out process. Rather, it was a serendipitous occurrence.

At that time, there was no effective treatment for tuberculosis. One antibiotic, streptomycin, was effective, but because it caused eighth-nerve damage, resulting in permanent deafness, it was discontinued. Another drug, isoniazid, was found to be effective.

It was noticed that many patients taking isoniazid were euphoric, and it was found that isoniazid improved people's moods. Biochemists began working with the chemical, and eventually the first effective antidepressant was developed.

This resulted in a major shift in psychiatric thinking. Until then, depression was attributed to emotional deprivation, especially in childhood. Now it became evident that certain chemicals could cause depression and/or relieve depression. A drug that helped control high blood pressure, Serpasil, caused severe depression. The pendulum swung to the opposite side. Mood disorders were not the result of life events, but were due to biochemical changes.

I can personally testify to this. In my second year of psychiatric training, I developed a severe depression that worsened over several weeks. I could not concentrate, I could not retain what I read, things that used to interest me no longer did, my appetite was gone, and I could not sleep. I consulted one of my professors who asked, "Abe, are you taking any medications?" I told him I was taking an over-the-counter decongestant for hay fever. "Stop the medication and let's see what happens." I did so, and after one week, all the symptoms of depression had cleared. Later that year, there was an article in the *American Journal of Psychiatry* that said decongestants may have a side effect of depression.

This ushered in an era of psychopharmacology. Some psychiatrists focus only on chemical treatment and relegate psychological treatment to psychologists. Several schools of psychology are in vogue. Each has something to offer.

During my years of active treatment, I was preoccupied with trying to help patients and didn't have the leisure to philosophize. Also, I became heavily involved in treatment of alcoholism and drug addiction, which provided insights into human behavior. I am now at a vantage point of assessing the phenomenon of discontent as it manifests itself clinically.

I am convinced that biochemistry is responsible for a number of psychiatric symptoms, especially mood disorders, panic attacks, and OCD. This does not mean they are not amenable to psychotherapy. Each therapist must evaluate what the most effective treatment is.

Although there is little doubt as to the role of biochemistry in some psychiatric disorders, there is at this time no laboratory test that can show the presence of the biochemical problem. Many patients present with depressive symptoms, and the tendency is to treat them with an antidepressant. As one prominent psychiatrist said, "If the only tool the carpenter has in his toolbox is a hammer, everything looks like a nail." There is nothing wrong with this, but one must remember that this is a supposition, and by no means have other factors been ruled out. Furthermore, we cannot dismiss the possibility of a placebo effect.

There are cases of "refractory depression," where all known physical modalities, including electrostimulation, have been utilized, with no improvement.

I think that some cases of depression are essentially due to chronic dissatisfaction. This is understandable in people whose living circumstances are of deprivation of one kind or another. But I've been around long enough to see people of great wealth, who could have whatever their hearts desire materially, who are physically in good health, who appear to have a caring family, depressed or driven to drugs. They do not respond to medication or to psychotherapy. There is no reason for them to feel deprived.

Prior to medical school, I was a pulpit rabbi for several years. When I graduated medical school, I made a resolution that I would not preach religion, and I have essentially adhered to that resolution. But religion is one thing and spirituality is another.

On several occasions in this book, I have referred to menschhood. I believe that a person who is physically healthy and is not impoverished may nevertheless experience chronic discontent if he has not exercised the unique human traits that distinguish man from other living things. I refer to this as "Spirituality Deficiency Syndrome." It may be misinterpreted as "depression," but neither medication nor traditional psychotherapy will help. He needs to be a full mensch, not a homo sapiens.

We live in an era of consumerism. There is a massive industry whose goal is to convince us that we *must* have the very latest apparatus on the market. People may have a smartphone that works perfectly, but if it's announced that a new, advanced model is on sale, there may be a line two blocks long of people ready to spend several hundred dollars for a gadget that actually does not offer much more than the model they have. The attitude is that if they don't have this very latest model, they are deprived. Given the inventive genius, there is always something one feels one is lacking. Rarely does acquisition of the new model result in more than a temporary good feeling.

I think there is an innate feeling of dissatisfaction, and we try to quell that feeling with anything that appeals to us, but it's insatiable. It's much like a person who is very hungry who will try to eat anything, even if it does not relieve his hunger for more than a few minutes. Drug addictions and alcoholism are examples of insatiable desires, sometimes resulting in irrational behavior. There is a quip about an alcoholic who saw a sign on a tavern, "Grand Opening! All the Booze You Want for $1!" He rushed into the bar and said, "Give me two dollars' worth!"

I don't want to violate my resolution to not preach religion, but I cannot refrain from conveying a statement I have heard many times from young people who recovered from drug addiction. They say, "When I stopped using drugs, I began to be aware of my feelings. I found that there was an empty space within me, and that was the space where God belonged."

This insight is of tremendous importance. Everything in the world is finite except for God, Who is infinite. If we wish to have a relationship with God, we must realize that this is an infinite quest. We can do things that will bring us closer to God, but, by nature, the quest can never be satisfied. To the contrary, the closer we come to God, the more we realize how distant we are from Him. Nevertheless, that should not be a frustrating experience.

A disciple of the Baal Shem Tov complained to the master that he was frustrated because his efforts to become closer to Hashem seemed to be counterproductive. The Baal Shem Tov told him the following parable.

"A father had an infant son he wanted to teach how to walk. When the child was able to stand upright, the father placed himself close to the child and extended his arms to within several inches of him. Until now, the child had ambulated on all fours, and he was fearful of taking a step forward. However, inasmuch as the father's hands were just inches away, the child had the courage to take the first step. The father then retreated a bit and beckoned to the child. Having successfully taken a step without falling, and still seeing the father close by, the child ventured two steps. Again the father retreated, and this continued until the child was able to walk.

"Think of what was going through the child's mind. *What is going on here? The more I try to reach my father, the further away he goes!* The fact is that the father and the child have two disparate goals. The child's goal is to reach the father, but the father's goal is to teach the child how to walk independently. If the father allows the child to reach him, the lesson is over."

The Baal Shem Tov said to his disciple, "You want to reach

Hashem. That is your goal. Hashem's goal is for you to grow spiritually. If He allows you to reach Him, your growth stops."

If we realize that our quest to reach Hashem is infinite and that is how it should be, we are not frustrated. But if instead of growing spiritually we feel frustrated, we are at risk of trying to fill the void, the space where God belongs, with earthly, material pleasures of all sorts, and this is doomed to failure. Whether it is alcohol, drugs, gambling, or food, it's a bottomless pit.

The Baal Shem Tov told his disciple that he should not feel frustrated because the spiritual growth in trying to reach Hashem is indeed infinite, but the goal *is the process, not the end point.* If we can grasp this, happiness is within our reach. If we do not understand this, we can be victims of chronic discontent, and our efforts to escape the chronic discontent may be seriously counterproductive.

Neither psychotherapy nor medication can relieve the frustration of trying to reach the infinite by finite methods.

Chronic discontent may contribute to depression, but there is a type of discontent that is actually beneficial. The Talmud is very critical of envy, which Shlomo HaMelech says is "the rot of the bones" (*Mishlei* 14:30). Envy is a worthless, destructive feeling, producing nothing but heartache. Yet there is one variety of envy that is praiseworthy, and that is *kinas sofrim*, to be envious of Torah scholars, because that stimulates a person to Torah study. By the same token, if a person is discontented because his knowledge of Torah is limited, that can encourage him to increase his Torah knowledge. This kind of discontent does not result in depression.

Negative envy can be a major obstacle to success and happiness. You have to get it out of your way.

Control

I don't know of any personality trait as ruinous as *control*. I have seen beautiful marriages destroyed by one spouse trying to assert control over the other spouse. What is worse is that the controller may not even be aware that he/she is controlling.

Control is not a uniquely human trait. Animals have a "pecking order," and one of the herd may be more powerful and assume a position of leadership. This animalistic trait should have no place in marriage.

I used to think that control was a defensive maneuver utilized by people suffering from low self-esteem to feel better about themselves. I have found a statement by the thirteenth-century Rabbeinu Yona of Gerona that *ga'avah* is a desperate maneuver to overcome feelings of low self-esteem. If a person can think himself superior to others, that soothes his pain of feeling inadequate and unworthy. I thought that the lust for power is a similar defense against low self-esteem, but the fact that it is present in animals, too, makes me think it may be a biological rather than purely psychological drive.

Marriage is not the only relationship affected by control. Parent/child, teacher/student, employer/employee are likely to be affected by control. There are situations where control is necessary, such as parents over small children who are unable to make proper decisions. But one must keep the control to the bare minimum necessary.

The efficacy of control is in the awareness that defying the control will result in negative consequences, i.e., control is based on the fear of reprisal. Fear and love are incompatible. Control breeds resentment, not love. The relationship with Hashem is the only one in which *yirah* and *ahavah* complement each other. In human relationships, the two are as opposite as fire and water. If one wishes to be loved, one should not seek to wield control.

A controller may be in total denial, just as the alcoholic is in denial of his dependence on alcohol. Exerting control may be as vital to him as alcohol is to the alcoholic. People who are being controlled may be unable to see this because it might jeopardize the relationship. There are cases where the husband's control is tyrannical, but the wife refuses to recognize this because she is dependent on her husband. People occupying positions of authority may not realize that they are controllers.

I am eternally grateful to a patient who put me in my place. I was walking along the corridor of a locked unit in the mental hospital, and I was jingling my keys. One patient said to me, "You have the keys to the door, and I don't. You can leave whenever you wish, and I can't. You don't have to remind me of it." I had no idea I was being insensitive and that by jingling the keys I was demeaning her while flaunting my authority.

People may use money as a means of control. Parents who support their newlywed children may feel this gives them the right to dictate to the children. Certainly, these parents wish to be loved, and they should be aware that control breeds resentment rather than love.

It was pointed out to me that the way one controls a horse is by pulling on the reins. This causes the horse pain, and it will turn in order to relieve the pain. Controlling others by intimidation is essentially treating them as if they were horses, which is certainly not going to endear you to them.

Parents have the obligation to teach their children proper behavior. Small infants may not be capable of absorbing principles of propriety, and parents may have to exert control. Rabbi Shlomo Wolbe, author of *Alei Shur*, says that *parents should learn how to discipline a child in a manner that will result in an inner desire to do what is right.*

This gives me an opportunity to share with you my favorite childhood memory, which I cherish and which gives me much warmth almost eighty years later.

Our living quarters were on the second floor, and the first floor was my father's shul. This was in the 1930s, and most *mispallelim* were first-generation immigrants from Russia and Poland. Several were hucksters, who collected paper and scrap metal with their horse and wagon. Late afternoon, they would put the horse in the barn and come to shul for *minchah*. While waiting for *minchah* to begin, they would drink hot tea in the kitchen and play chess. At age six, I watched them play and learned the game quickly. Soon I began beating the older players. At age nine, I was unbeatable.

One Rosh Hashanah, a rabbi from Chicago was our guest. In the afternoon, he invited me to play chess with him. "But it's *yom tov*," I said. The rabbi assured me that playing chess is not a violation of *yom tov*. I played him two games and beat him soundly.

The second night of Rosh Hashanah, I was summoned to my father's study. My father was studying a *sefer*, and I stood there waiting to be recognized. After a few moments, my father looked up from his *sefer* and said, "You played chess on Rosh Hashanah?"

"Rabbi C. said it was permissible," I said.

My father didn't say a single word. His eyes went back to the *sefer*, and he shook his head ever so slightly, but enough that I should understand that one does not play games on Rosh Hashanah, even if it is technically permissible. Rabbi C. was correct that it was not a violation of halachah, but it was not in keeping with the solemn nature of the day. Even at age nine, I got the message.

But I could not leave the room until he dismissed me with, *"Geh gezunterheit"* (Go in good health). He let me absorb the message a few minutes, then my father looked up from his *sefer* with a twinkle in his eyes. "Did you beat him?" he asked.

"Twice," I said.

He nodded with a smile and said, *"Geh gezunterheit."*

What genius method of parenting! He had to discipline me and let me know that I had done wrong, but *he was not going to allow me to leave the room feeling badly about myself.*

This is the trick of good parenting. Children must be corrected when they do something wrong, but they must not be made to feel bad. Over the last seventy-eight years I have never played even a permissible game on Shabbos or *yom tov*, but I was not made to feel guilty. Not too many people have warm, pleasant memories about being disciplined. I am fortunate.

Emunah

The Talmud says that sinful people are full of regrets. If a person who has *emunah* makes a reasonable investment that goes bad, he can say, "This is Hashem's wish. His judgment is far superior to mine." He does not torment himself with, "Why didn't I choose something more secure?!" A disbeliever, however, has no peace of mind, constantly castigating himself for having erred. Disbelievers torment themselves with regrets.

A person who has no trust in Hashem will try to manipulate things as if they were under his control. This invariably ends in frustration.

Emunah is, of course, the foundation of Yiddishkeit. The fact that the Jewish People have historically had problems in *emunah* requires that we understand why, and also what we can do to strengthen our *emunah*.

The Talmud says that Moshe Rabbeinu instructed us with 611 mitzvos, and that the first two mitzvos, "I am the Lord, your God" and "You shall have no other God before Me," were given to us directly by Hashem. David HaMelech said that all the mitzvos could be encompassed by eleven principles. The prophet Yeshayahu said they could be encompassed by six principles. The prophet Michah said by three principles. The prophet Chavakuk summarized them into a single principle, "The righteous shall live by his *emunah*" (*Makkos* 24a). *Emunah* is all-inclusive.

Just what is *emunah*? There are two aspects to *emunah*: (1) God exists, and (2) God is in control of the world.

To believe that God exists is not a major challenge. Anyone with a modicum of intelligence will recognize that our complex world, whose structure and functioning is mind-boggling, could not have occurred as a freak accident. More and more scientists are coming around to believe in Creation. The reluctance to accept Creation can best be explained by a dialogue between Rabbi Yehudah HaNasi and the Roman satrap, Antoninus.

Rabbi Yehudah said that the *yetzer hara* enters one at the very moment of conception. Antoninus said that's impossible, because if the fetus had a *yetzer hara*, it would kick its way out of the womb. Therefore, it must be that the *yetzer hara* enters at birth. Rabbi Yehudah conceded that Antoninus was right (*Sanhedrin* 91b).

The *mussar* authorities ask: Why would the fetus kick its way out of the womb? It has no concept of the lure of earthly pleasures. Furthermore, leaving the womb is certain death. They explain that the thrust of the *yetzer hara* is not as much the pursuit of pleasure as it is *the refusal to be restricted or restrained*. If the fetus had a *yetzer hara*, it would leave the womb, choosing certain death rather than being confined. The desire to be free and independent and the resistance to authority is manifest even in infants. As we grow, this attitude tends to increase in intensity.

Awareness that God exists can be experienced as a threat to one's independence and free will. A person may, therefore, find comfort in believing that God doesn't exist. Moshe Rabbeinu said that the sinful person may adopt this attitude, saying, "Peace will be with me, though I walk as my heart sees fit" (*Devarim* 29:18).

A physician who specializes in infertility said, "I was once peering through the microscope at a single cell — a fertilized ovum — and I realized that henceforth this tiny cell will get only carbon, oxygen, nitrogen, hydrogen, and few trace metals, and from that it will build a full human being! At that point I realized there must be a God."

Some people who cannot deny Creation preserve their attitude of independence by saying that while God did indeed create the universe, He abandoned it because it was beneath the dignity of an omniscient and omnipotent Creator to be concerned with mere earthlings. God, therefore, took off and left the operation of the world to underlings. Rambam says this is how *avodah zarah* began, when people began to worship natural or spiritual forces, which they represented by idols.

The major challenge in *emunah* is not in the belief in the existence of God, but rather in *hashgachah* — that God is interested and cares about the world and everything in it.

This is why the first of the Ten Commandments is, "I am the Lord, your God, Who took you out of the land of Egypt." Rav Simcha Bunim of Peshischa asks, "Why did Hashem not say, "I am the Lord, your God, Who created the universe?" It is because every sincere, intelligent person is aware of that. The problem is to believe that God is interested in the world and is in complete control of the world. This was proven by the miraculous Exodus from Egypt.

The belief that everything happens only because Hashem wills it, which is the first of the Thirteen Principles of Faith, is much more difficult to accept than belief in the existence of God. We understand Hashem to be absolute kindness and infinitely merciful, yet there are so many things that we observe that can cause a person to doubt this. There are so many things that conflict with our understanding of kindness and mercy that one may conclude that God is not in charge of the world.

Indeed, the Talmud says that Moshe asked Hashem why righteous people may suffer, and Hashem told him that this is something he cannot understand as long as he inhabits a physical body (*Berachos* 7a).

We are frequently challenged with this question. Why are some children born with defects that will cause them and their parents to live a life of suffering? Why do some patently sinful people prosper, while some righteous people may be deprived of the essentials of life? Why are there hurricanes, tornadoes, and tsunamis that bring grief to thousands of people? These and similar questions may challenge our belief in *hashgachah*. The answers that some people offer do not satisfy us. Logic fails us.

Like every other person, I am subject to these questions, and I am not satisfied by apologetics. In my study, I have a picture of my great-grandfather, Zeide Reb Motele, who was a great tzaddik, a phenomenal Torah scholar, and a great thinker. I am certain that every question that occurs to me certainly occurred to him. Yet, his *emunah* in *hashgachah* was firm and unyielding. It is absolute folly to think myself wiser than Zeide Reb Motele. If he believed in *hashgachah* in spite of the many challenges to it, that is more than adequate reason for me to believe.

To think of oneself as wiser than the great minds of the past is arrogance of the worst kind.

I had the privilege of being under the tutelage of a phenomenal Torah genius, whose encyclopedic knowledge and profound understanding of Talmud was mind-boggling. Yet he totally effaced himself before the earlier scholars — Rav Chaim Soloveitchik of Brisk, Rav Akiva Eiger, the Gaon of Vilna — who in turn totally effaced themselves before their predecessors, and so on to the Sages of the Talmud. I think of myself as hardly being a faintly lit match held in front of a 2,000,000-candlepower searchlight. Standing in utter awe of these spiritual giants, who knew all the challenges that may occur to me, I must surrender to their incomparably greater wisdom. If *emunah* was good enough for them, it's good enough for me.

For me, the all-encompassing principle of the *navi* Chavakuk, "The righteous shall live by his *emunah*" (2:4) is based on my appreciation of the greatness of our tzaddikim. Yet it is even presumptuous of me to think that I can appreciate their greatness. Rav Moshe Sofer (the Chasam Sofer) was one of the greatest Talmudic scholars of recent history. He was a student of Rav Nosson Adler. His son, Rav Shimon Sofer, a great Torah scholar in his own right, wrote that his father's teacher, Rav Nosson Adler, was "indeed a Heavenly angel." The Chasam Sofer was outraged, saying, "No Heavenly angel could possibly reach the heights of the Master."

The Torah says that at the miracle of *krias Yam Suf*, "the people had faith in Hashem and in Moshe, His servant" (*Shemos* 14:31). The *Mechilta* comments, "This verse teaches us that having faith in the leader of Israel is equivalent to having faith in Hashem."

Recognizing the superiority of the minds of our great tzaddikim and their unwavering faith and trust in Hashem enables me to have *emunah*.

That does not mean that we have no questions. We are

only human, and we cannot help but wonder why some things occur.

Rav Avraham Yaakov of Sadigura said, "When my brother, the Rebbe of Chortkov, recites Tehillim, Hashem says, 'Dovidl, I am turning the world over to you. You may do with it whatever you wish.' My brother's *emunah* in Hashem's justice is so complete that he returns the world to Hashem as he received it. If Hashem would make that offer to me, I would make some changes."

Rav Avraham Yaakov certainly had *emunah*, yet given the opportunity, he would make some changes. *Emunah* may not eliminate our questions. *Emunah* enables us to have faith and trust in Hashem in spite of our questions.

For me, the key to *emunah* is the appreciation of the superiority of the minds of our tzaddikim, which so dwarf my mind that I can share in their *emunah*.

How do we achieve an appreciation of the greatness of tzaddikim? Through stories!

Are all the stories we are told about our tzaddikim true? My friend Rav Berel Wein addresses that question with this story.

> *The Chafetz Chaim was asked to testify as a character witness in a case, and was instructed to take the oath to tell the truth. As the Chafetz Chaim never took oaths, he asked to be excused. The lawyer said to the judge, "This rabbi does not need to take an oath. He is physically incapable of lying.*
>
> *"Let me tell Your Honor something about the character of this rabbi. He once saw a thief make off with his silver candlesticks, and in order that the thief not be guilty of the sin of theft, the Chafetz Chaim declared them hefker, i.e., he relinquished his ownership of them."*

The judge said, "Do you expect me to believe that?"

The lawyer responded, "Your Honor, they don't tell stories like that about me or you."

The stories about tzaddikim do not have to be factual to be true.

Stories are the most effective method of communication. Stories can communicate what is generally invisible and ultimately inexpressible. Stories provide a perspective that touches on the Divine, giving shape and form even to the invisible.

Some of the stories may be old, but even old stories become "new" to us when something in our own experience makes us ready to hear them.

I have heard the Torah reading of the saga of Yosef and his brothers every year for the past eighty years, yet it's always new. Every year, when I hear how Yosef reveals his identify, saying, "I am your brother Yosef, whom you sold into slavery," I get a lump in my throat the size of a grapefruit and my tears begin to flow. As old as the story is, it has a fresh element every year that connects with a part of me that had previously been untouched.

Hearing is more than reception of sound waves. We need to be ready to hear. All therapists have had the experience of a client saying, "I've been coming here for the past two years. Why haven't you pointed this out to me before?" We *had* pointed "this" out to the client countless times, but the client was not ready to hear it before. Yes, you may have heard some of the stories I will relate, but they may now touch you in a way that makes them "new."

A man asked the *gaon* Rav Chaim Kanievsky how to teach his son *yiras Shamayim*. Rav Chaim suggested *sifrei mussar*. The man asked, "Is that how your father (the Steipler Gaon) taught you?" Rav Chaim said, "He told me *sippurei tzaddikim* (stories of tzaddikim)."

Some people say that the stories told about tzaddikim may be self-defeating, because they place the tzaddikim on a superhuman level, so lofty that we cannot possibly identify with them. That isn't true. The tzaddikim were very much human, but they were great human beings. We are fortunate to have had people who knew the Chafetz Chaim. He was a true human being, not a mythical figure. I was privileged to have a personal relationship with the Steipler Gaon, a person whose every move was guided by halachah. I also knew Rav Shlomo Zalman Auerbach, a great tzaddik of unparalleled halachic stature, but whose *middos* exceeded even his voluminous Torah knowledge.

I hope you will share with me the *emunah* that can be gained from the stories about our tzaddikim.

Which Way to Emunah?

The Torah literature on *emunah* cites two ways to achieve *emunah*. David HaMelech said to his son, "Know the God of your forefathers and serve Him" (*Divrei HaYamim I* 28:9). To "know" God implies having an awareness of God via philosophical reasoning, but the term "God of your forefathers" implies awareness of God via acceptance of tradition, of transmission of the belief in God from generation to generation.

The *sefarim* point out the pros and cons of each way. The philosophical understanding may be very profound, but there is a risk that someone may come up with an argument that disproves your conclusion. Acceptance by tradition may be more superficial, but it is unlikely to be disproven by arguments to the contrary.

There were indeed great tzaddikim like Rambam, Yehudah HaLevi, Yosef Albo, and others, who were philosophers. The consensus of most authorities is that one should have a firm, unshakable *emunah* based on tradition before engaging in philosophical speculations about Hashem.

As I indicated, my *emunah* is based primarily on the testimony of our great tzaddikim. The fact is that this is how we conduct ourselves in our daily lives, relying on the endorsements of competent and knowledgeable people when we must make important decisions. A person who needs open-heart surgery will seek out the opinions of the most knowledgeable people he can find about the qualifications of the surgeon who is going to open his heart. He will seek out the best endorsements for a procedure that puts his very life in the hands of the surgeon. One may also seek the opinion of a competent auto-mechanic on which car to buy.

Of course, there are foolish endorsements. A beer maker will have a famous athlete endorse his beer. But what makes an athlete a maven on beer? Why should his expertise in sports qualify him in the taste of beer? His taste may not agree with mine, and I see no logical reason why I should drink the beer he likes.

The endorsements for my *emunah* are from tzaddikim who were qualified in *emunah* and who were devoid of self-interest: my *zeide* Reb Motele, the Chafetz Chaim, the Vilna Gaon, the Baal Shem Tov, the Chasam Sofer, Rav Akiva Eiger, etc., all the way back to the Sages of the Talmud and the *nevi'im*. Anyone who has even the slightest appreciation for their incomparable greatness should have no problem with *emunah*.

The stories I will present describe the greatness of the tzaddikim, their vast Torah knowledge, their impeccable *middos*, and their relentless pursuit of truth. Their lives were an endorsement of *emunah* that can satisfy all the doubts my mind can generate.

In 1965, I met Rabbi Kaplan, the chief rabbi of Tzfas, who related the following story.

> "As a bachur, I attended the Mir Yeshivah, and I boarded with a family. One Friday morning, the husband left to buy provisions for Shabbos, and the wife called after him, 'Be sure to be back early.'

When I returned for lunch, the wife was standing in the doorway, anxiously looking for her husband.

"I said, 'Why are you so anxious? There is still plenty time until Shabbos.'

"The wife said, 'I'll tell you why. After we were married, we had no children for several years, and then Hashem blessed us with a son. But the child was not developing well, and we took him to the doctor, who said, "Take the child to the heart specialist in Vilna." The heart specialist examined the child and said, "Take the child home. There is nothing I can do for him."

'I returned to the hotel where I was lodging, and cried. A woman who was there asked why I was crying, and I told her that this is my only child, and the doctor has given me no hope. The woman said, "On your way home, stop off in Radin and get a berachah from the Chafetz Chaim."

'In Radin, I was told that the Chafetz Chaim was very old and frail, and was not receiving anyone. I was crushed, but then I saw a young man, the Chafetz Chaim's grandson, who had boarded with us when he was at Mir. I begged him to get me in to see his grandfather.

'When I met the Chafetz Chaim, I burst into tears. The Chafetz Chaim said, "Don't cry, my child. Tell me your trouble." I explained my plight, and the Chafetz Chaim said, "Promise me that every Friday you will have the table set for Shabbos before noon, with the candles ready for lighting. You will be very careful to light the candles long before sunset. Hashem should give your child a refuah."

'Of course, I promised, and I kept my promise. My child began to develop well. I took him back to the local doctor, who said, "Were you at the clinic in Leipzig?" I told him that I had been to the heart specialist in Vilna. The doctor said, "Take the child back to the doctor in Vilna."

'The heart specialist examined the child and said, "This is not the child you brought to me before."

'I said, "This is my only child."

'The doctor said, "What did you do for the child?"

'I said, "I received a berachah from the Chafetz Chaim."

'The doctor, who was a nonobservant Jew, said, "I didn't want to tell you how bad it was. Your child's heart was completely failing. As doctors, there are times we can do something for an ailing heart. But to remove a completely diseased heart and replace it with a healthy heart, only the Chafetz Chaim could do that."'

"The woman said, 'Now you may understand why I am so anxious that my husband return early.'"

The Vilna Gaon was once in his sukkah and was, as usual, engrossed in Torah study. A man came in to see him, but the Gaon was so absorbed in Torah that he wasn't aware of him. The man waited a while, then left. Later, the man said to the Gaon, "Why did you ignore me in the sukkah?"

The Gaon said, "Heaven forbid that I would ignore you. You are very dear to me. I was so occupied in my study that I wasn't aware that you came in. Please forgive me. Hashem should bless you to live to be one hundred."

When the man was ninety-eight, he fell sick, and the family wished to call a doctor. The man said, "There is no need for a doctor. I am going to get well. The Gaon promised me I would live to one hundred." Indeed, after his one hundredth birthday, the man died.

Whereas we may question the veracity of ancient stories, first-person stories are more convincing.

When my uncle, the Bobover Rebbe, Rav Shlomo Halberstam, died, the family was sitting shivah. A stranger, accompanied by a young boy, walked in, sat down, and burst into tears. The family had never seen this man before.

The man said, "My son here was diagnosed with a malignant disease, and the doctors gave us little hope. I was taking my son to the doctor's office, when my wife said, "Why don't you stop off at the Bobover Rebbe for a blessing?" I am not an observant Jew, and I have no contact with Rebbes, but my wife insisted, and to placate her, I visited the Bobover Rebbe.

When I told the Rebbe about my son's serious condition, the Rebbe took the child, felt his body in several places, then said, "I don't understand. I can't see anything wrong." He then blessed the child to have good health.

I thanked the Rebbe, but I didn't make much of it.

In the office, the doctor examined the child and appeared bewildered. "I don't understand. I can't see anything wrong" (The Rebbe's very words). "I'll repeat the X-rays." After the X-rays were read, the doctor said, "I'm stymied. I don't see any sign of the disease."

"That was four years ago. Here is my child, in good health thanks to the Rebbe's blessing."

I was privileged to be under my uncle's tutelage for a year. He survived the Holocaust, lost his wife and two children, and witnessed the unspeakable horrors of the Holocaust. Yet, his emunah was unshakable, and he began to rebuild some of the Yiddishkeit that Hitler had destroyed.

That is a source of my emunah.

In the town of Nadvorna, the Rebbe built his sukkah. The mayor of the town was a virulent anti-Semite and ordered the Rebbe to take down the sukkah. The Rebbe said, "This sukkah was meant to last for eight days, and so it will be."

The mayor sent repeated warnings, and when the Rebbe ignored them, he came personally to confront the Rebbe. "I order you to dismantle that hut," he said.

The Rebbe said, "My uncle was Rebbe Meir of Premishlan."

The mayor said, "I don't care who your uncle was. That hut must come down now!"

"Just listen to me," the Rebbe said. "There was a nobleman who had several fruit trees, and he had the trees cut down to plant a flower garden. He had a number of children, but one after another, they died. Doctors could not explain the cause of their deaths.

"There was one surviving child, and the townsfolk said, 'In Premishlan, there is a Wunder Rabbiner, a rabbi who accomplishes great things. Consult him. Perhaps he can tell you how to save your last child.'

"The nobleman went to Premishlan, and Rebbe Meir told him, 'The Torah forbids cutting down a fruit tree. Because you violated that and destroyed viable fruit, God punished you to lose your "fruit," your children.' But Rebbe Meir gave him a blessing that his last child would survive."

The Rebbe continued, "You, Mr. Mayor, are that surviving child. Your life was spared by a blessing of my uncle. And this is how you are rewarding him?"

The mayor began to cry. "I know the story to be true. I apologize for my rudeness. No one will disturb any Jew in this town who puts up a hut for the holiday."

Obstacles to Emunah

"For, inquire now regarding the early days that preceded you, from the day that Hashem created man on the earth and from one end of Heaven to the other end of Heaven: Has there ever been anything like this great thing or has anything like it been heard? Has a people ever heard the voice of God speaking from the midst of the fire as you have heard?" (*Devarim* 4:32).

"Has anything like it been heard?" Is there another nation that has an unbroken chain of transmission of an event *witnessed by three million people*?

One might ask, "How can there be a denial of *emunah*?" The answer lies in the understanding of *avodah zarah*. The Israelites witnessed the miraculous phenomenon, seeing the sea split before their very eyes, yet one man, Michah, brought his idol along from Egypt and carried it through the divided sea! (*Sanhedrin* 103b). Can one think of a greater, more absurd paradox than this? That is the power of *avodah zarah*.

The Talmud says that we have no concept of the lure of *avodah zarah* in ancient times. King Menasheh was an idolater who brought an idol into the Beis HaMikdash. He appeared to the Sage Rav Ashi in a dream and said, "Had you lived in my time, you would have lifted your coattails and run after the *avodah zarah*" (*Sanhedrin* 102b). The Sages successfully prayed to curtail the seductive power of *avodah zarah*.

The Talmud says that the Israelites never really believed in the *avodah zarah*. They used the *avodah zarah* to legitimize their prurient drives. This principle still prevails. People who have forbidden desires seek to "kasher" them by adopting authorities who will approve of them.

The latter is a major obstacle to *emunah*. The Rebbe of Kotzk said, "There are no *apikorsim* today. There are only *baalei ta'avah* who seek positive sanction for their forbidden desires."

The Torah says that a bribe will "blind the eyes of the wise and distort the words of the righteous" (*Devarim* 16:19). A strong craving for something will "bribe" a person so that even a wise person's judgment is corrupted. Our tzaddikim, who subdued their physical cravings, were able to achieve profound *emunah*. To the extent that we can free ourselves of the dominance of our earthly desires, to that degree can we develop *emunah*.

Emunah is an intellectual exercise. We may not be aware that most of our behavior is *not* based on use of our intellect.

In *Alei Shur* (vol. 1, pp.155-157), Rav Shlomo Wolbe makes the startling statement that the exercise of *bechirah*, true free choice, is a rare phenomenon. We think of *bechirah* as a uniquely human trait. Animals do not have *bechirah*. Animals function according to instincts. A hungry jackal that spies a carcass being fed on by a ferocious tiger does not attempt to eat from it. Its hunger instinct is overcome by its instinct for survival. It knows that if it attempts to take food away from the tiger, the tiger will kill it. Similarly, if a child who knows she will be punished for raiding the cookie jar resists the temptation, this is not *bechirah*, but merely the fact that the fear of punishment exceeds her desire for the cookies.

Rav Wolbe points out that much of our behavior is determined by habit, by the desire to please others, or by similar motivations.

A person who has no control over his anger is a slave to it. A person whose greed drives him to make money is a slave to it. A person who does things to get *kavod* is a slave to it. A person who feels he must do things to please others is a slave. None of these behaviors is really *bechirah*. Rav Wolbe says that a person may live a long life *without exercising bechirah even once*!

As was noted, a person may resist *emunah* because he feels it obligates him and stands in the way of gratifying his desires. When this person says the Shema and accepts upon himself *Ol Malchus Shamayim* — choosing to follow the dictates of Hashem rather than his own desires — that is *bechirah*.

True *bechirah* — rather than acting according to the strongest instinct — is uniquely human.

It is related that a tzaddik who was aware of a poor family gave them *tzedakah*. He later returned and gave them some more money. He explained, "When I initially gave them money, it was not really for the mitzvah of *tzedakah*. I felt the pain of seeing them hungry, and I gave them money to relieve my discomfort. I later returned to give them *tzedakah* for the mitzvah, rather than to placate myself."

The Aderes (Eliyahu David Rabinovitch-Teomim) was known for his punctuality. When his daughter died and the funeral was set for 11 a.m., people gathered at his home at that hour. They were surprised when the Aderes did not appear at the appointed time. In fact, it was five hours before he came out.

The Aderes later explained, "The Talmud requires that when one suffers a serious loss, one must recite the blessing, Baruch Dayan Emes. The Talmud further states that one should recite this berachah with simchah (Berachos 59b). Rashi explains that simchah in this context does not mean joy, but rather 'with one's entire heart,' i.e., with complete faith in the justice of Hashem's judgment."

The Aderes continued, "I did not feel that I could recite the berachah with the requisite emunah. I had to meditate for several hours until I could achieve the sincerity to recite the berachah properly. That is why I was late for the funeral."

Our tzaddikim worked hard to have *emunah*. Our tzaddikim achieved *emunah* by perfecting their *middos*.

Rav Moshe Kramer of Vilna was a great Torah scholar who was appointed Rav of Vilna. He stipulated that he would not accept a salary, but would support himself by a small grocery that his wife operated.

The people of Vilna, who wanted to provide for their rav in a more abundant way, would overpay for the items they bought in their rav's grocery. When Rav Moshe noticed that there was more money in the house than he expected, he investigated and discovered that the customers were overpaying.

So Rav Moshe calculated exactly how much money they needed for the week and told his wife that when that amount had been earned, she was to close the store. "There are other grocers in Vilna who also need to earn a living."

The Chafetz Chaim acted similarly, instructing his wife to close their store at noon. When customers then made all their purchases in the morning, the Chafetz Chaim had her close the front door.

"The neighbors know there is a rear entrance. Other customers can patronize the other groceries."

Our tzaddikim had emunah that Hashem would provide for their needs.

The Chafetz Chaim once lodged at an inn, and the innkeeper got into a discussion with him, expressing his skepticism of the miracles related in the Torah. "Why don't we have such miracles today?"

Instead of getting into a discussion with him, the Chafetz Chaim said, "I will answer your question before I leave."

Later that day, the innkeeper's daughter returned from school and proudly displayed the certificate she'd received for coming in first in a contest for memorizing poetry. The Chafetz Chaim asked, "Could you please recite for me some of the poems you memorized?"

The young girl said, "No."

The innkeeper said, "Why don't you recite some poems for the rabbi?"

The young girl said, "Here is the certificate that I know the poems by heart. If the rabbi doesn't want to believe the certificate, he doesn't have to. I don't have to perform for everyone."

The Chafetz Chaim said to the innkeeper, "There you have the answer to your question. Hashem did great miracles to show that He controls the world. Then He gave us a certificate, the Torah, which states this for all generations to come. Like your daughter, He does not have to perform for everyone."

The Chafetz Chaim could have told the innkeeper that we all experience Hashem's miracles every day, as we say in the Amidah, but he knew that this would not satisfy the innkeeper's skepticism. Instead, he waited for an opportunity that would be more impressive.

But how did the Chafetz Chaim know in advance that such an incident would occur? He had *emunah* that since the innkeeper had challenged him with the question, Hashem would provide him with the ability to give him a satisfactory answer.

That is *emunah*.

Emunah is Truth

Truth is a rare commodity. Unfortunately, our culture operates on the principle of *expedience*. Whatever best serves our purposes is assumed to be true. Modern society is hardly ready to make significant sacrifices for the truth.

We have an amazing capacity to rationalize, i.e., to convince ourselves that what we *want* to be true is indeed true. In forty-plus years of treating addictions, I became aware of how common it is to convince ourselves of what we prefer to believe. I wrote a book about it, *Addictive Thinking: Understanding Self-Deception*.

Rationalization, which is nothing but self-deception, is not limited to addiction. It's a very common phenomenon. Not only do you believe what you want to believe, but you can come up with "evidence" to support your position. You can actually fabricate such evidence and swear that it is true. It is worthwhile knowing the following incident to become aware of how our minds can deceive us.

In 1968, Dr. Herbert Spiegel, a renowned psychiatrist who specialized in hypnosis, collaborated with NBC reporter Frank McGee, in the following: They asked a thirty-four-year-old man, who appeared to be in perfect mental health, to participate in an experiment. He was assured there would be no residual effects from this.

Dr. Spiegel hypnotized the man, and said, "I am going to give you an important piece of information, and at some point, I will show you a sheet of paper with some names. To end the hypnotic session, I will tap your left shoulder. You will come out of the trance and think you heard a joke."

Dr. Spiegel said, "The important information I want you to know is that there is a Communist conspiracy to infiltrate the media and spread Communist doctrine to the American people. Now you can open your eyes and talk with us while remaining in the hypnotic trance."

The subject opened his eyes and, after a few moments, said to Frank McGee, "There is something important you should know as anchor of NBC news. The TV media are being infiltrated by Communists, and they will be spreading Communist ideas to the whole country."

Frank McGee said, "That is a serious accusation. Why should I believe it?"

The subject said, "I know what I'm talking about. I attended some meetings where this was being planned."

Frank McGee said, "Where were those meetings held?"

The subject said, "On the second floor over an abandoned theater on Fourteenth street." He then went on to describe the theater and the proceedings at the meeting.

McGee asked him, "Was Paul Harris one of the attendees?"

The subject said, "No."

McGee then showed him a blank sheet of paper, saying, "Were any of these people there?"

The subject studied the blank sheet, and said some of the names listed were there. "Bill Harris was there. I never thought he would participate in this. He is a loyal army veteran."

The session continued, with the subject providing

"evidence" about this conspiracy. McGee said, "I think you're making this up."

The subject became angry, saying, "No, it's true, and it's a great danger to the country."

Dr. Spiegel then touched the subject's left shoulder. He emerged from the trance, smiling. He had no memory of what had transpired.

This session was filmed. When the subject saw the film, he was aghast. "I never knew anything about a conspiracy. I never was at 14th street. I don't know anyone named Harris. I don't know where I got all the 'facts' I quoted."

This is a powerful demonstration that if a person has an idea, he will vigorously defend it, fabricating "evidence" to support his idea. *Nothing can budge a person from an idea that he believes to be true,* such as a psychotic person who believes himself to be Mashiach.

If a person has a need to deny the existence of God and/or *hashgachah*, nothing may be able to change his mind. What is generally referred to as "truth" is actually what a person wishes to believe.

Shlomo HaMelech declares, "Do not rely on your own understanding" (*Mishlei* 3:5). Inasmuch as we conduct our lives based on what we believe, we must be most cautious about what we believe to be true.

The Pursuit of Truth

Rav Eliyahu Eliezer Dessler, in *Michtav Mei'Eliyahu*, has an important essay on "The Perspective of Truth." We noted that the Torah says that a bribe can completely distort one's perception and judgment. Rav Dessler says that any personal interest is essentially a bribe, hence it is extremely difficult for a person to be objective. The only way to avoid such distortion is to be free of personal interest, which is almost impossible.

David HaMelech lists eleven points that are essential to be close to Hashem. "One who walks in perfect innocence, and does what is right, and speaks the truth in his heart; who has no slander on his tongue, who has done his fellow no evil, nor cast disgrace upon his close one; in whose eyes a contemptible person is repulsive, but who honors those who fear Hashem; who can swear to his detriment without retracting; who lends not his money on interest; nor takes a bribe against the innocent" (*Tehillim* 15:2-5).

The Talmud gives an example of "speaking the truth in one's heart." Rav Safra was praying when someone approached him, offering a sum of money for an item he wished to sell. Rav Safra could not interrupt his prayers, and remained silent. The customer assumed the silence to be a refusal of the amount he had offered, so he increased the offer. Again, Rav Safra remained silent, and the customer continued increasing his offer. When Rav Safra finished his prayers, he told the customer he would sell him the item for the first offer he had made. "I could not respond to you, but since in my heart I had agreed to accept that amount, I must keep to that" (*Makkos* 24a, Rashi).

Rav Chaim Shmuelevitz cites the incident (*Vayikra* 10:16-20) where, following the deaths of Aharon's two sons at the dedication of the Mishkan, Moshe Rabbeinu told Aharon and his two remaining sons that although they were mourners, who generally may not eat the meat of the offerings, Hashem specifically instructed that they may do so today.

In addition to the offerings of the dedication, there was also the offering of Rosh Chodesh, which Aharon's sons burned. Moshe was angry at them, telling them that Hashem had instructed him that they may eat the sacrificial meat even though they were mourners. Aharon said to Moshe, "Hashem did indeed tell you that they may eat of the offerings of the dedication, but did He also say that they may eat of other offerings?" Moshe said, "You were right. Hashem said as you said, but I forgot."

Rav Shmuelevitz points out that Moshe had a dilemma. He was the only conduit of Hashem to us. If he admits that he forgot what Hashem said, that puts the entire Torah in jeopardy. People may say, "If Moshe is capable of forgetting what Hashem said, how can we know that everything else he said is authentic from Hashem?" Perhaps it would be better for him to have said, "Follow my instructions as I gave them to you," rather than cast doubt on the authenticity of the Torah forever.

Rav Shmuelevitz says that Moshe decided, "Preserving the authenticity of the Torah is not my responsibility. Telling the truth *is* my responsibility. I must tell the truth that I forgot what Hashem said, and let the consequences be whatever they may be."

> *Rav Chaim of Volozhin said that one must have utmost respect for one's teachers. Nevertheless, if a student feels that the teacher is wrong, he should respectfully seek to clarify it, but not accept it as correct. "Truth must prevail over all."*
>
> *Rav Yisrael of Salant was delivering a Torah lecture, and someone in the audience challenged a point he had made. Rav Yisrael thought for several moments and then admitted that the challenge was right. He then alighted from the pulpit.*
>
> *Later he said, "I could have rebutted the challenge in five different convincing ways, but I did not feel that they were true. I was debating with myself that perhaps for kavod haTorah I should rebut his challenge. Then I said to myself, 'Yisrael! Yisrael! What have you learned in mussar? Where is your dedication to the truth?' So I admitted I was wrong and left the bimah."*

Levels of Emunah

Believing that Hashem created the world is just the first step of *emunah*.

Torah begins with the account of Creation. Prior to Creation, there was nothing in existence except God. The Torah teaching is that God created the universe *ex nihilo*, out of nothingness. This phenomenon is certainly in defiance of all laws of nature. Anything that occurs against the laws of nature can exist only as long as there is a force to maintain its existence, otherwise it reverts to its natural state. For example, the law of gravity dictates that a rock lying on the ground will not lift off the ground unless there is a force stronger than the gravitational force that keeps it on the ground. If someone throws the rock into the air, it will remain aloft only to the extent of the force that propelled it. When that force is exhausted, the rock returns to its natural place, on the ground.

Inasmuch as creating something out of nothing is against the laws of nature, it follows that the universe can continue only as long as there is a force maintaining its existence. If such a force were to be withdrawn, the universe would immediately return to the natural pre-Creation state: nothingness.

The Alter Rebbe, author of the *Tanya*, states, therefore,

that the Divine utterances that brought the universe into existence were not a onetime thing, but are ongoing, and it is these utterances that maintain the existence of the universe. This is the meaning of the verse, "Forever, Hashem, Your word stands firm in Heaven" (*Tehillim* 119:89).

Although the Torah refers to the Divine utterances of Creation as verbal commands, i.e., "God said," that is because we have no other way of grasping a command. However, God does not speak as humans do. Just as words reveal a person's thoughts, the phrase "Hashem said" is used to describe the Divine Will. The "utterances" were emanations of Godliness that brought into being and gave form to everything in the universe. Everything that exists does so only because of the nucleus of Godliness within it that maintains it. *If the nucleus of Godliness were withdrawn, the object would cease to exist.*

Although we can have no concept of the Divine essence, we use whatever words we possess to refer to Godly attributes, with full realization that these are inaccurate and are essentially parabolic. Thus, the Torah says, "May God illuminate His countenance for you" (*Bamidbar* 6:25), and in the Amidah we refer to "the light of Your Countenance." The Divine blessings are conceived of as emanations of His light. Inasmuch as the Divine emanations share in God's infinity, their "light" is infinitely great.

If one held a lit match in front of a searchlight that had a million-watt illumination, the flame of the match would not be detectable, because it would be obscured by the overwhelmingly greater light of the searchlight. Similarly, if the nucleus of Godliness that is of infinite "brightness" and that is within everything in existence were visible to the human eye, it would so obscure everything that nothing in existence could be visible.

This can be extended even further. The flame of the match obscured by the powerful searchlight nevertheless does have an independent existence. It's just that it cannot be seen because it is overpowered by the much greater light of the searchlight. However, objects in creation don't have an independent existence. Their entire existence is the word of God, shielded in such a manner that we perceive them as independent objects.

Because it is His wish that there be a physical world that will enable a person to do mitzvos, God so shielded the nucleus of Divinity in everything so that physical objects are visible to us (much as one can look at the sun only through heavily smoked glass). However, if we could perceive the real truth of existence, i.e., the Divine nucleus that maintains objects in existence, the objects themselves would not exist for us.

(It is jokingly related that a group of Chabad chassidim were discussing this chassidic philosophy deep into one Friday night, long after the candles had extinguished. They were focusing on the teaching that the only true existence is God. On the way out of the shul in the darkness, one chassid collided with the wood-burning stove, sustaining a blow to his forehead. He remarked, "Even if nothing in the world exists, the stove for sure exists.")

There are thus two "realities": (1) the *true* reality, which is that God is the only being in the universe, and (2) the reality that God wishes us to perceive, in which there are physical objects that enable us to carry out the Divine Will of performing the mitzvos. This is a reality in which God's presence is obscured, but one must know that all that we can see and touch is totally dependent on God for its existence.

A rebbe was sitting with several of his chassidim, and asked, "Do you believe in God?"

They were taken aback and said, "Of course we believe in God."

The rebbe said, "Well, I don't believe in God."

The chassidim were stunned. Then the rebbe asked, "Do you believe that this is a table, or do you know it is a table? There is no need to believe in something you see. You know it is there. Similarly, I don't believe in God because I know He exists."

Great *tzaddikim* knew that everything in existence is sustained by a Divine nucleus within it. We must believe it.

Rav Dov of Radshitz lodged at an inn. In the morning, he asked the innkeeper, "Where did you get the chime clock?" The innkeeper told him that there was a guest who could not pay his bill, and left the chime clock as a pledge.

"Do you know whether this guest was in any way related to the Rebbe of Lublin?" Rav Dov asked.

The innkeeper said, "Now that you mention it, I think he did say something about the Rebbe of Lublin."

"I knew it!" Rav Dov said. "Every time I heard the chime, I felt an urge to get up and dance. You see, a chime clock is actually a very depressing instrument. Every time it chimes, it reminds you that another segment of your life is irretrievably gone. Not so the clock of the Rebbe of Lublin. Every chime meant that we are a bit closer to the coming of Mashiach."

Emunah in the coming of Mashiach can convert sadness into joy.

To Learn from Everyone

The Talmud says, "Who is a wise person? Someone who learns from everyone" (*Pirkei Avos* 4:1). I am not wise, but perhaps if I try to learn from everyone, I may yet become wise. In my more than forty years of treating alcoholics, I learned many things. Yes, even about *emunah*.

I'm sure you've had days when Murphy's Law was in full swing. Anything that can go wrong, did. These are days when we realize we would have been better off pulling the covers over our heads and staying in bed till 4 p.m.

I had a morning like that in Manhattan. Flat tire, stopped by a police officer for driving ten miles above the limit, couldn't find an open parking lot, etc. By noon I was fit to be tied. I felt that the only thing that could get me out of the quicksand was an AA meeting. A call to the local AA office produced no less than four meetings within a six-block radius.

The speaker was a young woman of thirty-five. She had started drinking at age twelve and drugging at fifteen. This led to delinquent, decadent behavior. In spite of suffering the consequences of living on the street, she was a slave to her drug addiction.

At twenty-six she found her way into Alcoholics Anonymous and Narcotics Anonymous, and at present was nine years clean and sober.

I had heard similar stories countless times, and this one did little for me. But I have never been to a meeting from which I didn't take away something of value. What I took away from this meeting has served me well.

Toward the end of her talk, the woman said, "I must tell you something else before I finish. I am a football fan, a rabid Jets fan. I'll never miss watching a Jets game. One weekend I had to be away, so I asked a friend to record the game on her VCR. When I returned, she handed me the tape and said, 'By the way, the Jets won.'

"I started watching the tape, and it was just horrible! The Jets were being mauled. At halftime they were behind by twenty points. Under other circumstances, I would have been a nervous wreck. I would have been pacing the floor and raiding the refrigerator. But I was perfectly calm, because I knew they were going to win.

"Ever since I turned my life over to God, I no longer get uptight when things don't go my way. I may be twenty points behind at halftime, but I know it's going to turn out okay in the end."

I had yet another lesson. It was one of those days when I awoke in the morning feeling down, for no identifiable reason. In the afternoon, I was standing in front of my house watering the lawn when a car pulled up to the curb and two guys jumped out. They were alumni of my Gateway treatment center.

"Hi, Doc," one said. "How ya doin'?"

"If you guys weren't in the program, I would say 'Just fine.' But I don't lie to people in the program. I've had a lousy day."

"You need a meeting, Doc," they said.

"No, thank you," I said. "I'll be all right."

That night the doorbell rang. It was these two guys. "We're

here to take you to a meeting," they said.

Just my luck to end up at a "gratitude meeting." Everyone who spoke gave a brief account of how much happier they are in their sobriety. When you feel depressed, the last thing you need is to hear how happy other people are. I sat patiently through the meeting, hoping it would soon be over.

The last speaker said, "I am four years sober, and I wish I could say that they have been good years. My company downsized, and I was let go. I have been unable to find a job. My marriage was on shaky grounds anyway, and this was the clincher. My wife divorced me and got custody of the children.

"My house was foreclosed because I was unable to make the mortgage payments. Last week the finance company repossessed my car. But I can't believe that God brought me all this way just to walk out on me now."

In the *Nishmas* prayer there is a verse, "Your mercies have supported me until now, and I know that You will never abandon me." I had been saying that prayer regularly for over eighty years, but I had never before felt it the way I did after this meeting.

We're often confronted with challenges, some of which may appear to be overwhelming. If we reflect a bit, we will recall that we have weathered challenges in the past that we thought were overwhelming, yet we survived. That should give us the courage and confidence to cope with the present challenge.

> *The Baal Shem Tov was traveling in an unpopulated area with a student, who said, "Master, I am very thirsty, but there is no water here." The Baal Shem Tov remained silent. After a bit, the student said, "Master, if I don't get water soon, I may die."*

> *The Baal Shem Tov said, "Do you believe that when Hashem created the world, He foresaw everything, including your present thirst, and provided for it?"*
>
> *The student was silent. After meditating a bit, he said, "Holy Master, I believe it."*
>
> *The Baal Shem Tov said, "Then just wait a bit."*
>
> *After a few moments, they saw a peasant carrying two buckets of water. The Baal Shem Tov beckoned to him, gave him a few coins, and gave the thirsty student some water.*
>
> *The Baal Shem Tov asked the peasant, "Why are you carrying water in this unpopulated area?"*
>
> *The peasant replied, "The poritz I work for has gone out of his mind. We have a well on the premises, but he sent me to fetch water from this distant well for no good reason."*
>
> *The Baal Shem Tov said to the student, "This teaches you what hashgachah pratis is. Hashem caused the poritz to go mad in order to provide water for you."*

The Apter Rav (*Ohev Yisrael, Noach*) said that in addition to meaning "belief," *emunah* also has another meaning: to "raise" or to "bring up." He cites the verse in *Megillas Esther* (2:7), "*Vayehi omein es Hadassah*," where *omein* means to raise. The Apter Rav says that with profound *emunah* one can actually bring about something, which may explain the appearance of the water in this story.

Our National Weakness

The Midrash says that before Hashem gave the Torah to Israel, He offered it to other nations, who rejected it. He offered the Torah to the Edomites, descendants of Eisav, who asked, "What does the Torah say?"

Hashem said, "It says, 'You shall not kill.'"

The Edomites said, "We cannot accept the Torah. Our forefather, Eisav, was blessed to live by the sword" (*Bereishis* 27:40).

Hashem offered the Torah to the Moabites, who said, "What does the Torah say?" Hashem said, "It says, 'You shall not commit adultery.'"

The Moabites said, "We cannot accept the Torah. Our very existence is based on immorality" (*Bereishis* 19:30-38).

The commentaries explain that the reason Hashem offered the Torah to other nations is because when the Israelites will be elevated and rewarded at the final Redemption, the other nations might complain that had they been given the Torah, they, too, would have merited Paradise. Inasmuch as they rejected it and only Israel accepted it, they will have no grounds for complaint.

Rav Yitzchak Meir of Gur commented, "The other nations might still complain. They may say, 'You told us that the Torah forbids killing and immorality. But to the Jews you said that the Torah requires belief in "I am the Lord, your God." Had You told that to us, we would have accepted it.'"

Rav Yitzchak Meir said, "The goal of Torah is to enable a person to overcome one's natural inclinations in order to achieve spirituality. Therefore, Hashem told the Edomites and Moabites that the Torah forbids killing and immorality because that is their weakness. These are not the weaknesses of the Jews. The Jewish nation is neither murderous nor lustful. Our weakness is that we are skeptics. We have great difficulty believing in God. Even after witnessing the great miracles of the ten plagues in Egypt, the splitting of the sea, and the daily portion of the *mahn, am Yisrael* still tested Hashem, saying, 'Is Hashem among us or not?' (*Shemos* 17:7). Therefore, Hashem presented the Torah to Israel by addressing Israel's fundamental weakness. Hashem said, 'I am the Lord, your God. Can you accept that?'"

This is an important insight. The prophets railed against idolatry, but their words fell on deaf ears. Jews could not commit themselves to Hashem, which resulted in the loss of our homeland and the destruction of the Beis HaMikdash.

Humility

Humility was the hallmark of our tzaddikim.

The Chida (Rav Chaim Yosef David Azulai) relates that beneath the study of the Maharshal (Rav Shlomo Luria) there was a vegetable store, whose proprietor was a man named Avraham, a very quiet, unassuming person. One night the Maharshal awoke and heard Avraham studying a very difficult passage of the Talmud, elucidating it with ingenious insights. He realized that Avraham was a great scholar who was concealing his vast Torah knowledge.

The Maharshal sent a messenger to ask Avraham a question in halachah. Avraham told the messenger that he must be mistaken, because he knows nothing about halachah.

The Maharshal then confronted Avraham and, by the authority of being the rav of the town, ordered him to reveal the truth about himself. Avraham had no choice, but pleaded with the Maharshal not to expose him. The two great scholars then became chaveirim, studying Torah together.

Before his death, the Maharshal left instructions that Avraham, proprietor of the vegetable store, succeed him as Rav, because there was no one who could equal his mastery of Torah. Only after unrelenting pressure of the townsfolk did Rav Avraham yield and assume the position of Rav.

The Indestructible Spark

Historians recorded that during the Spanish Inquisition, when Jews were forced to convert to Christianity or be killed, many Jews accepted martyrdom rather than relinquish their allegiance to Hashem. Among them were Jews who were not observant of Torah and mitzvos, yet they chose to die rather than renounce Hashem.

The Baal HaTanya explains this as a spark of Yiddishkeit that exists even in nonobservant Jews. He says that while Jews do not want to relinquish their bond to Hashem, they are under the impression that transgressing the mitzvos doesn't sever that bond. However, when put to the test of renouncing Hashem, which would sever their relationship to Him, they choose rather to die.

The *Tanya* says that this indestructible spark of loyalty to Hashem is a bequest from Avraham Avinu to everyone who has a Jewish *neshamah*. Our indulgence in physicality and material pleasures prevents this nucleus of holiness from becoming manifest.

Chassidic writers refer to this nucleus of holiness as being in *galus*, trapped within a physical body and unable to exorcise itself.

Rav Hillel of Paritch once noticed a man in shul crying after he had finished davening. Rav Hillel asked the man whether he had suffered an adversity. The man said, "No, I am crying for the pain of my neshamah. It has come down from its place in Heaven, and it's trapped within a physical body that craves so many things that are anathema to the neshamah."

The *Zohar* says that when Hashem "breathed" a spirit of life into man, He instilled something of Himself into man. This *neshamah* seeks to bond with its Source, but the physical body and mind are obstacles. If we pursue spiritual rather than physical goals, we relieve the *neshamah* of its distress.

Emunah in Hashem's Absolute Kindness

The Torah relates that when Moshe carried Hashem's message to Pharaoh to send out *bnei Yisrael*, Pharaoh reacted by intensifying their enslavement. Moshe complained to Hashem, "Why have You done evil to this people?" (*Shemos* 5:22). Rashi says that Moshe was punished for this.

But why? Isn't it the mission of the Jewish leader to be an advocate for his people? Wasn't Moshe supposed to complain to Hashem that their suffering had worsened?

The Chafetz Chaim said, "Of course. But Moshe used the wrong words. He should have known that Hashem never does evil. If a person experiences distress, he may say that it is 'bitter,' but not bad. A lifesaving medication may taste bitter, but it's actually very good."

> *During the lifetime of the Maggid of Mezritch, there were no harsh anti-Semitic decrees, but they recurred after his death. One of the Maggid's disciples wondered, "Inasmuch as tzaddikim are even greater after their death than during their lifetimes (Chulin 7b), why is the Maggid not annulling these harsh decrees now?"*
>
> *The Maggid appeared to him in a dream and said, "When I was on earth and I saw a harsh decree, I prayed to Hashem to annul*

it. Now, from my vantage point in Heaven, I can see the ultimate good of these decrees. I cannot annul something that is ultimately good. You, on earth, who see these decrees as bad, you can pray to annul them."

When we recite the Shema, we cover our eyes. We do so because we assert that "Hashem," which represents the Divine attribute of *chesed*, and "Elokeinu," which represents the attribute of harsh judgment, are both "Hashem," i.e., kindness. But we don't see it that way. We cannot see the good and the kindness in distressful experiences. We therefore cover our eyes as a symbolic statement that our human vision is fallible, and that all that emanates from Hashem, the unpleasant as well as the pleasant, is all *chesed*.

Emunah means believing that Hashem is absolute kindness. It requires belief, because our human minds don't perceive this.

Hashem Will Provide

We often verbalize that, "Hashem will provide," but our *emunah* is not always strong enough for us to take courageous steps based on this belief. Our *gedolim* had real *emunah*.

In Prague, there was a Torah scholar, Rav Zerach Eidlitz, who had once competed with the Noda B'Yehudah for the position as Rav of Prague.

Rav Zerach, formerly a man of means, lost all his money and was being pressured by his creditors. He confided his plight to the Noda B'Yehudah.

"How much are you in debt?" the latter asked.

"Three thousand dinars," Rav Zerach replied.

The Noda B'Yehudah had been saving up money for his daughter's wedding. He went to his strongbox and found that he had three thousand dinars, which he gave to Rav Zerach.

Several days later, the Noda B'Yehudah's wife opened the strongbox and was shocked to find it empty. The Noda B'Yehudah told her that he had lent the money to Rav Zerach. "What did you do?" she said. "Everyone knows that Rav Zerach is bankrupt."

The Noda B'Yehudah said, "Rav Zerach is a God-fearing person. He will never renege on a loan."

As the wedding day approached, the Noda B'Yehudah was asked to give his opinion about a din Torah involving an estate of a very wealthy man. The Noda B'Yehuda suggested terms for a settlement. All the litigants were pleased, and they paid him three thousand dinars for his services.

Did the Noda B'Yehuda have *emunah* that the three thousand dinars he lent Rav Zerach would be restored? I don't know. But I do know that when he gave Rav Zerach the three thousand dinars he had saved up, he had *emunah* that he was doing the right thing.

The Teaching of the Mahn

The chassidic master, Rav Mendel of Rimanov, said that the provision of the *mahn* in the desert was a necessary prerequisite for the giving of the Torah. A human being comes into the world as an animal and must learn to subdue its animalistic drives. The acquisitive drive, if not frank greed, is an inborn trait, as is envy. "An infant at birth has a clenched fist." Unless bridled, these traits do not permit a person to live an ethical and moral life.

The miracle of the *mahn* was not only that it was provided every day, but also that the amount a person received was fixed according to the number of people in his household. If a person gathered more than his due, the excess rotted. If one gathered less, the measures miraculously filled up. This enabled people to realize that Hashem would provide for their needs. It was now possible to give them a Torah that dictates, "You shall not steal" and "You shall not covet your fellow's belongings."

Without *emunah* in Hashem, the only thing that would restrain a person from taking the property of others is the fear of punishment if one is apprehended stealing. People may be clever enough to avoid being detected. The knowledge that one cannot exceed what was allotted by Hashem discourages giving free rein to selfish, acquisitive drives.

> *Rav Zusha of Anipol lived in abject poverty. He was asked, "How can you, in good faith, recite the berachah, "Blessed is Hashem Who has provided for all my needs" when you are lacking so much?"*
>
> *Rav Zusha replied, "Hashem knows what my needs are better than I do. He knows that one of my needs is poverty, so He has given it to me."*

With *emunah*, it's possible to have peace of mind.

Shevet Mussar (28) says that *resha'im* are full of regrets.

Rebbe Pinchas of Koretz explained that when a person who has *emunah*, who believes in Hashem and in *hashgachah pratis*, fails in some venture, he realizes that Hashem wanted this and that it's ultimately to his advantage. He has no regrets.

If a person who does not believe in Hashem, and who thinks he is in full control of his life, fails in some venture, he takes himself to task — "If I would have done things differently, I could have succeeded" — and eats his heart out. This person is full of regrets.

Righteous people aren't full of these kinds of regrets. They trust Hashem's wisdom. The only regrets righteous people have is if they deviated from observance of Torah, because that is something that Hashem doesn't control. Our ethical and moral decisions and behavior are a matter of free choice, which Hashem leaves to us.

Emunah in Hashem, Not in People

"Do not rely on nobles, nor on a human being… Praiseworthy is one whose help is the God of Yaakov" (Tehillim 146:3,5).

A chassid came to the Rebbe of Kotzk complaining that he needed to marry off his daughter but did not have the funds to do so. The Rebbe gave him a letter to a wealthy man, Rav Moshe Chaim Rottenberg, a brother of the Chiddushei HaRim, asking him to help the man.

When Rav Rottenberg read the letter, he gave a man a single ruble. The man was bitterly disappointed. "The very trip here cost me more than a ruble," he said, but Rav Rottenberg didn't budge.

The man left brokenhearted, and Rav Rottenberg sent someone to fetch him back. When he returned, Rav Rottenberg gave him a large sum of money, adequate for the wedding and for new clothes.

"I don't understand it," the man said. "Why did you first give me just one ruble?"

Rav Rottenberg said, "You came with a letter from the Rebbe, certain that I would give you all the money for the wedding. You were so sure of it that you lost trust in Hashem. When I gave you only a ruble, you could no longer rely on me, and so you had to pray to Hashem."

One should never forget that Hashem runs the world.

The Baal Shem Tov wanted a special wine from Bessarabia, and he sent a disciple, Rav David, to see that the wine was made with the most stringent precautions. Rav David never removed his supervision from the time of the grape harvest until it was sealed in the barrels.

Thrilled that he had satisfied the master's wishes, he brought the wine to the Baal Shem Tov's home. Just then, a government inspector, on the lookout for illegal spirits, came by and opened the barrel. Contact with a non-Jew rendered the wine nonkosher.

Rav David was devastated. All the effort he had invested to bring the master the wine he desired were rendered null in a single moment. Rav David asked the Baal Shem Tov why this had happened. He responded, "You went to such great extremes to make sure the wine would be kosher, that you forgot to ask for Hashem's help. We must remember that without Hashem's help, nothing we do can succeed."

Precursors to Emunah

I will betroth you to Me forever, and I will betroth you to Me with *tzedek, mishpat, chesed, and rachamim* (righteousness, justice, kindness, and mercy). I will betroth you to Me with *emunah*, and you shall know Hashem" (*Hoshea* 2:21-22).

We can have a relationship with Hashem if we desire that relationship to be eternal, if we exercise *tzedek, mishpat, chesed, and rachamim*, and only then will we achieve *emunah*.

The four traits cited are the essential precursors for *emunah*, and all require self-effacement. If a person lives a life of selfism, one cannot achieve these traits.

> *Rav Zusha of Anipol saved up enough money to have the tailor sew a dress for his wife. When she went to pick up the dress, she saw that the tailor was tearful. He said, "My daughter is soon to be married, and when she saw this dress, she assumed it was for her wedding. I don't have the heart to tell her it's not for her."*
>
> *Rav Zusha's wife said, "I can manage without a new dress. Give this dress to your daughter."*
>
> *When she related this to Rav Zusha, he said, "You had a great mitzvah to gladden the heart of a bride. But did you pay the tailor for his work?"*
>
> *"Pay him?" the wife said. "Why, I gave him the dress."*

> Rav Zusha said, "You hired him to sew the dress. That you decided to do a mitzvah and give him the dress for his daughter is very noble of you, but that does not discharge your obligation to pay him for the work he did."
>
> Rav Zusha's wife assumed that as she gave the tailor the dress, she did not have to pay him for his work. Rav Zusha told her that this is not tzedek.

> Rav Yehoshua Heshel Frenkel was Rav in Komarno. One day he overheard conversation in shul that the sons of the wealthy were able to buy their way out of conscription into the Polish army, but that there was a young man from a poor family who was going to be drafted. For a Jew to be in the Polish army was a death sentence because not only was his spiritual life in jeopardy, but also his physical life, at the hands of the Polish anti-Semites. However, there was no money to buy his freedom. "Furthermore," the people said, "he is a boor and isn't an asset to the community."
>
> When Rav Frenkel heard this, he became enraged. How can we allow a Jew to be in such peril? He opened the aron kodesh and said, "Holy Torah! You are the splendor of Israel. You do not need to be beautified by a silver crown. I am taking your crown and pawning it to save a Jewish life. When we raise enough money, we will return your crown to you." He indeed did so, and bought the young man's freedom.
>
> Rav Frenkel then said to the young man, "I pawned the Torah crown for your freedom. How will I save face if you know nothing of Torah?" He arranged for the young man to receive a Torah education, and he became a respected citizen of the community.

Was it right to pawn the Torah crown? Rav Frenkel's concept of *tzedek* saved a Jewish life.

We do practice kindness and mercy, but there are many levels of these. We look to our tzaddikim for direction.

Although we may not reach their level of *middos*, we can use their examples as guidelines.

> It was the practice of Rav Menachem Nachum of Horodna that when he was given the honor of being sandek at a bris, he would inquire about the family's economic situation, and when necessary, he would cover the expenses of the bris celebration and the needs of the mother and the infant.
>
> One time, a local storekeeper invited Rav Menachem Nachum to be sandek. Rav Menachem Nachum found out that the storekeeper was in difficult financial straits, but was too proud to accept help. He said to the storekeeper, "I have a friend in Warsaw who is sick, and needs financial help. Perhaps on your next trip to Warsaw on business you can give him these thirty rubles. I'd rather not send it by mail."
>
> The storekeeper said, "I don't have any plans to be in Warsaw soon."
>
> Rav Menachem Nachum said, "It's not an emergency. You can do it whenever you go. In the meantime, you can use the money, and whenever you'll be in Warsaw, you'll take care of it."
>
> The storekeeper made a proper seudah for the bris. After the bris, he said to Rav Menachem Nachum, "You didn't give me the address of your friend in Warsaw."
>
> Rav Menachem Nachum said, "You're right. I don't have it with me. I'll look it up and give it to you."
>
> Rav Menachem Nachum assiduously avoided meeting the storekeeper. If he did meet him, he thought of some excuse why he didn't have the address. Months later, the storekeeper's financial condition improved. He came to Rav Menachem Nachum and gave him the thirty rubles, saying, "Since you don't have the address, I'm returning the money."
>
> Rav Menachem Nachum had given the storekeeper a loan without impinging on his pride.

The Talmud is lavish in its praise of those who fulfill the mitzvah of *tzedakah,* yet states that the mitzvah of doing *chesed* surpasses even *tzedakah,* because *tzedakah* is done with one's possessions, whereas *chesed* is done with one's person (*Sukkah* 49b). But how far does one have to go to do *chesed*?

> *The Alter Rebbe (the author of the Tanya) had a chassid with five unmarried daughters. "Why aren't your daughters married?" the Rebbe asked.*
>
> *The chassid answered, "I am a poor melamed. I have no yichus. I am a nobody. Why would anyone want to do a shidduch with me?"*
>
> *The Alter Rebbe said, "I have a son, Berel (who became the Mittler Rebbe), who is a fine lamdan. I will take one of your daughters as a wife for him. You will be the Rebbe's mechutan, and people will be happy to do a shidduch with you." And so it was.*

How many people would make that sacrifice, doing a *shidduch* with someone who is far beneath their status and dignity, in order that this person's social status be elevated?

(Note: I'm proud that I'm a descendant of that *shidduch* of supreme *gemilus chasadim.*)

Tzedek, mishpat, chesed, and *rachamim* cannot be properly practiced by someone preoccupied with selfism. Personal interests warp one's sense of judgment and one's emotions. As the prophet says, without these precursors, one cannot achieve *emunah* and a closeness with Hashem.

A selfish person cannot truly believe in Hashem. He is too convinced that he is his own god. Self-worship is no less an *avodah zarah* than idol worship.

Rising from a Fall

I have often referred to insights I gathered working with alcoholics and drug addicts. In *Teshuvah Through Recovery* I capitalized on these.

Ricki was a young man who experienced the dredges of addiction. After recovery, he led an exemplary life. One day, his mother said to me, "Ricki is such a wonderful young man. What a shame that he had to go through the ugliness of drug addiction."

Ricki overheard his mother's remark and said, "You don't understand, Mom. I never could have become what I am now without going through that phase."

Rebbe Nachman of Breslov was vehement in arguing that one should never despair, regardless of how depraved one may have been. "Life consists of ascents and descents." The prophet Michah says, "Although I have fallen, I have arisen" (7:8), to which the commentaries note, "Had I not fallen, I would never have arisen."

While we certainly wish to avoid all negative behavior, we should realize that this is just not realistic. We've all had experiences we thought were very bad only to discover at a later date that it was a blessing in disguise. We have to use our best judgment and get the best counseling, but then we should leave the rest to Hashem.

Chassidic philosophy and Kabbalah offer explanations why some good things must pass through a transition of bad. These explanations are beyond my grasp. We must avoid letting negative happenings throw us into depression. Rebbe Aharon of Karlin said, "Nowhere does the Torah state that being depressed is a sin, but there is nothing that is as conducive to sin as being depressed."

The *yetzer hara* is wily and uses every possible strategy to disable a person. Under the guise of delivering *mussar*, the *yetzer hara* may cause a person to feel so guilty about the mistakes he has made that it saps his energy. Chassidic teachings are that we must always look for ways to find *simchah*.

I have often referred to the 12-step recovery meetings. It is characteristic at a meeting of Alcoholics Anonymous to hear recovering alcoholics relate their antics and crazy behavior of their drinking days, and everyone joins them in laughter. This is the strength of recovery. You do not allow the past to pull you down.

"One day at a time" has two meanings. It means to deal with the challenges of today, which is doable, rather than undertake the entire future, which is more than one can handle. "One day at a time" also means not to relive the past.

Hashem has given us the gift of *teshuvah*. If we have made mistakes, even serious mistakes, and we make amends and do proper *teshuvah*, Hashem erases those mistakes as though they never occurred.

Make every effort to have an upbeat, positive attitude. *Simchah* is a great mitzvah.

Chanan Got Outta His Way

Having discussed rising from a fall, I wish to share the story of Chanan. I will include all the details. I believe the message is uplifting.

On Purim night, after the Megillah, the phone rang. "Hi, Rabbi, this is Chanan. I'm calling to tell you that today marks thirty years since I walked into Gateway. It's been unbelievable. Hashem has been good to me."

Thirty years ago, I received a call from a rabbi in Chicago. A young man came to him for help with a severe drug problem. He was alienated from his family, and was penniless. The rabbi said he would try to raise some money for his treatment.

Chanan was twenty-seven. He came from a fine *frum* family. His father had *semichah*. Chanan had dropped out of his third year in college because of drugs. When his father refused to give him money for drugs, he got into a physical fight with his father, who threw him out of the house. He had nowhere to go and started wandering around the country. His shenanigans ended up in his being jailed in six different states.

Chanan was cooperative in the twenty-eight-day treatment

program. When he left, he found a minimum-wage job. He attended the recovery meetings faithfully. He made some extra money teaching kids their bar mitzvah *haftarah*.

After several months, I said to Chanan, "Okay, you're clean and sober. What are you going to do with the rest of your life?"

Chanan said, "I'm three credits away from getting my bachelor's degree. All I've got to do is write a paper to get my degree."

"So, go ahead and write the paper."

Chanan said, "Rabbi, my brain is so foggy that I can't even read a newspaper article."

I said, "Your brain looks good to me. Write the paper and show it to me. If it's not good, we'll wait a few months."

Several weeks later, Chanan said, "I didn't want to burden you, Rabbi. I wrote the paper and sent it in." A few weeks later, he was notified that he had been granted his bachelor's degree.

I said to Chanan, "Congratulations! Now what? What were your plans for after college?"

Chanan said, "I was thinking of law school."

"So let's go on from there," I said.

Chanan shook his head. "There's no way I could ever make it in law school."

I said, "Stop knocking yourself. Stop this negative thinking. You're bright and capable."

Several weeks later, Chanan said to me, "Rabbi, were you serious about my going to law school?" I told him that I was absolutely serious. He said, "I would have to take the Kaplan course to pass the LSAT exam. That course costs four hundred dollars, and I don't have it."

I said, "If you make the effort, I'll do the rest."

I then put in a few phone calls to lawyers who were in AA and asked them to help Chanan. Within a week we had the four hundred dollars. Chanan studied intensively and did remarkably well on the test. He applied and was accepted to a first-rate law school. But then he said, "I can't afford the tuition plus room and board plus books. I applied for a student loan but was turned down because I still owe seven thousand dollars from my college loan. I told the loan official that if I get this loan and go through law school, I'll repay this loan plus the seven thousand dollars. He agreed, but it was nixed by his superior."

I said, "Chanan, it's time you asked your father to help you."

Chanan said, "That's a waste of time, Rabbi. I know what he's going to say."

"You may be right, but do it anyway," I said.

The next day, Chanan told me that his father had screamed at him, "When did you think up this scheme to milk me for money for cocaine and heroin?!"

I told him to tell his father to call me, and that I would verify that he was genuine. Chanan called me the following day. His father said he wouldn't give him the money, but would lend it to him, and Chanan was admitted to law school.

Several months later, Chanan called me. "It was all a big mistake, Rabbi. Exams are coming up, and there's no way I can sit for exams. The drugs caused too much brain damage."

I told Chanan, "There you go with your negative attitude again. While you were studying, most of your fellow students were partying. You'll run circles around them."

A few weeks later, Chanan reported that the exam grades were posted, and he received two A's and a B. "But they didn't post the big exam grade. And I know that I flubbed that one." Three days later, Chanan reported that he received an A on the big exam. "I knew that they had made a mistake, so I checked it out with the professor, and it was no mistake."

I said, "Will that teach you to stop depreciating yourself?"

Chanan excelled so well that he got a scholarship for the second year. Eventually, he got a clerkship with a prestigious law firm. Chanan was now able to put to legitimate use all the manipulative shtick of his drug-using years. The law firm realized they had a gem in their midst, and he was hired after graduation.

Chanan married and has a wonderful family. Overcoming his character defects enabled Chanan to achieve an undreamed-of success.

He had gotten outta his way.

CONCLUSION

At the beginning of this book, I wrote that it is widely assumed that there are three essentials for human survival: (1) food and water, (2) clothing, and (3) shelter.

I then added a fourth: *someone to blame.*

Many things can go wrong in the course of normal living, and we invariably blame someone for them. If we can fault someone else for it, it absolves us from taking corrective steps. However, this allows the error to repeat itself.

The fact is that most often, as we have seen from this book, we ourselves are at fault.

This book encourages us to find the real culprit: ourselves. Accepting that there is no one to blame but ourselves makes it possible for us to correct our mistakes. We just have to be honest and brave enough to accept responsibility for our mistakes.

And if we can do that, we can get out of our own way.

The book that no suffering person or family should be without…

**Confused.
Desperate.
Trapped.**

Hear the voices of those most vulnerable: those addicted to alcohol, drugs, gambling, exposure to inappropriate material, and other destructive plagues of our times.

In this eye-opening book on teshuvah and recovery, renowned author and psychiatrist Rabbi Abraham J. Twerski offers his wise insights into the psychological and spiritual aspects of addiction and the benefits of joining a 12-step program. Included are inspiring personal accounts of those who have descended to the lowest recesses, yet emerged triumphant from the depths of darkness.

Available at your local Judaica store or at:
1-855-MENUCHA • www.menuchapublishers.com

More fascinating reading from
RABBI DR. ABRAHAM J. TWERSKI

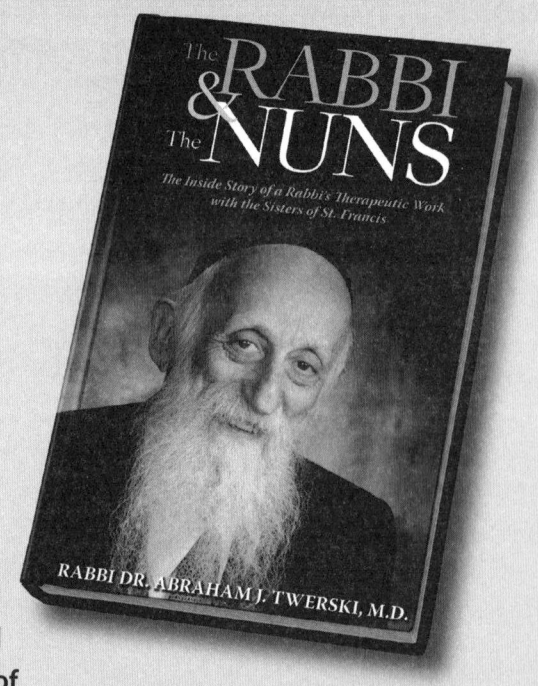

What happens when you take a Chassidic rabbi and make him director of psychiatry at a Catholic hospital?

You get a unique and utterly fascinating read!

The Rabbi and the Nuns: The Inside Story of a Rabbi's Therapeutic Work with the Sisters of St. Francis chronicles the highlights of a twenty-year working relationship between Rabbi Dr. Abraham J. Twerski and the nuns and priests of the Pittsburgh Diocese and St. Francis Hospital. Spearheading a groundbreaking rehab program, Rabbi Twerski and the nuns develop a working connection that transcends their religious differences, forges mutual respect, and brings them to a whole new level in ecumenical relations.

Available at your local Judaica store or at:
1-855-MENUCHA • www.menuchapublishers.com